Enigmatic If Not Ineffable

Enigmatic If Not Ineffable

Studies in Philosophy

ROBERT SAMUEL THORPE

WIPF & STOCK · Eugene, Oregon

ENIGMATIC IF NOT INEFFABLE
Studies in Philosophy

Copyright © 2019 Robert Samuel Thorpe. All rights reserved. Except for brief quotations in critical publications or reviews, no part of this book may be reproduced in any manner without prior written permission from the publisher. Write: Permissions, Wipf and Stock Publishers, 199 W. 8th Ave., Suite 3, Eugene, OR 97401.

Wipf & Stock
An Imprint of Wipf and Stock Publishers
199 W. 8th Ave., Suite 3
Eugene, OR 97401

www.wipfandstock.com

PAPERBACK ISBN: 978-1-5326-7963-6
HARDCOVER ISBN: 978-1-5326-7964-3
EBOOK ISBN: 978-1-5326-7965-0

Manufactured in the U.S.A.   APRIL 15, 2019

Contents

Preface | vii
Acknowledgements | ix

1	T.H. Huxley's Problem with the Cosmic Process	1
2	The Foundation of Morality	31
3	Xenophanes' Concept of God	41
4	Seneca and Virtue	48
5	The Case Against Science	51
6	Imaginationism	61
7	The Nature of Faith	66
8	What Does It Take to Build a World?	73

Appendix | 77
Bibliography | 103

Preface

PHILOSOPHY LENDS ITSELF TO thinking, so a book of thoughts should be a likely result. Not only are there thoughts in this book, but they are somewhat scattered among several subjects—also a tendency of philosophers. Certainly, thought should pop into the philosopher's mind frequently and precipitate a mystical investigation of possibilities, stimulating the imagination, and provoking the cognitive machinery. Such are these mental wanderings which have resulted in some coherent conclusions and some others which have been left in the desert parts of the mind for future contemplation. Americans have shamefully ignored this kind of exercise, in the classrooms of public schools, even in required classes for college degrees, by our focus on the economic success of the sciences and mathematics. But without the training of our thoughts, we fail to solve human and social problems in our worlds and content ourselves to live in an intellectual environment devoid of consistency and truth. Post-modernism, with all its supposed tolerance, ignores reality for the sake of self-indulgence and self-justification. There is truth; the law of contradiction is true; revelation is an avenue of epistemology; Jesus Christ is truth embodied—the Word of God incarnate. Think on these things.

ROBERT SAMUEL THORPE
March 2013

Acknowledgements

To my sweet wife, Chrissy and my wonderful children, James, John, Ben, and Anna, all of whom have always been supportive, encouraging, and patient with Dad's struggles and endeavors, I give my most profound and tender love and appreciation. God bless all of you in the richest ways.

To Oral Roberts University, students and colleagues, who have provided me with many reasons to write and teach the truth as I understand it. God bless you as well.

1

T.H. Huxley's Problem with the Cosmic Process

THOMAS H. HUXLEY, RENOWN advocate and promoter of Charles Darwin's theory of evolutionary biology, gave a lecture in 1893 entitled "Evolution and Ethics." This speech was subsequently published by the Macmillan Company and reproduced in a volume entitled *Readings in Philosophy* edited by John Herman Randall, Jr., Justus Buchler, and Evelyn U. Shirk[1]. Though perhaps mentioned in other speeches or writings, Huxley's idea in this lecture, that the "cosmic process," or Darwinian macro-evolution, reveals itself to be deficient in certain ways, stimulated my thinking that perhaps he had put his finger on a major logical issue with the accepted notions of modern science in relation to ethics.

Furthermore, if Darwinian evolution cannot explain or justify "civilized" ethical philosophy, according to Huxley, then what issues are then left unresolved by evolutionary thinking?

Huxley evidently supported the notion of Darwinian evolution, i.e., the survival of the fittest by natural selection, as the "cosmic process," the force and method of the development of life on earth. "From the very low forms up to the highest, the process

---

1. Randall, Buchler, and Shirk, *Readings in Philosophy*, 222–38. See Appendix for the text of the speech.

Enigmatic If Not Ineffable

of life presents the same appearance of cyclical evolution.[2] In every part, at every moment, the state of the cosmos is the expression of a transitory adjustment of contending forces, a scene of strife, in which all the combatants fall in turn. What is true of each part is true of the whole. Thus the most obvious attribute of the cosmos is its impermanence. It assumes the aspect not so much of a permanent entity as of a changeful process in which naught endures save the flow of energy and the rational order which pervades it."[3] In the midst of this changing universe we know now that the universe is expanding and demonstrates entropy rather than a permanent consistent strength. A "cyclical" appearance of nature has not been demonstrated, especially in extinct species and apparent environmental destruction. There are some aspects of the whole which is not true of the parts. Some species cannot cope with change while others revel in it.

The notion that the universe has existed so long that a lengthy process of change has resulted in the complex systems of life we now observe has been reconsidered. Stephen Jay Gould, a prominent evolutionist, concluded that the universe could not have been in existence eternally, but in fact, for not very long.

> If the universe had existed for eternity, and had always contained the same number of stars and galaxies as it does today, distributed in more or less the same way throughout space, it could not possibly present the appearance we observe. Stars pouring out their energy, in the form of light, for eternity, would have filled up the space between themselves with light, and the whole sky would blaze with the brightness of the sun. The fact that the sky is dark at night is evidence that he universe we live in is changing, and has not always been as it is today. Stars and galaxies have *not* existed for an eternity, but have come into existence relatively recently; there has not been time for them to fill the gaps in between with light.[4]

2. Huxley, "Evolution and Ethics," 222.
3. Huxley, "Evolution and Ethics," 223.
4. Gould, *Eight Little Piggies*, 5–6.

T.H. Huxley's Problem with the Cosmic Process

Gould indicates that the idea of a cosmic process must be conceived without the necessity of vast eons of time, since the universe "relatively recently" existed, and within the universe is the earth, which had to develop in an even shorter period of time. So any idea of an evolutionary process of development must be considered to be much shorter than initially believed. This shorter historical development throws some doubt into the effect of a cosmic process at all. Teilhard's understanding is more logically acceptable, that "the scientific idea of evolution implies no more that the affirmation of this fact: that every object and every event in the world has an antecedent which conditions its appearance among other phenomena."[5] Though somewhat Platonic, Teilhard only insists that there may be a process whereby all things develop and change. In this notion, Huxley may be clearer as he said, "the cosmos is the expression of a transitory adjustment of contending forces."

Huxley supported the view that humankind developed within the process of natural selection and rose to the top of the food chain, as it were. "Man, the animal, has worked his way to the headship of the sentient world in virtue of his success in the struggle for existence" because of conditions and organization better than his competitors.[6] "In the case of mankind, the self-assertion, the unscrupulous seizing upon all that can be grasped, the tenacious holding of all that can be kept, which constitute the struggle for existence, have answered."[7] The reason humans could rise so high was due to the nature of the human personality and drive. Man's great characteristics that have enabled him to survive in the cosmic process of strife against competition, i.e., his "exceptional physical organization, his cunning, his sociability, his curiosity, and his imitativeness, his ruthless and ferocious destructiveness . . . against opposition, have now become defects." "Man now punishes many of the acts which flow from them [ape and tiger] as crimes."[8]

5. Teilhard, *Science and Christ*, 192.
6. Huxley, "Evolution and Ethics," 223.
7. Huxley, "Evolution and Ethics," 223.
8. Huxley, "Evolution and Ethics," 224.

Enigmatic If Not Ineffable

There seems to be no clear evidence that any species of animal has ever "worked its way up" the ladder of evolutionary structure. In most natural ways, humans are one of the least "fittest." We do not breed in great numbers; our physical strength and endurance are obviously inferior to many other animals; without artificial environments, we are more affected by environment that many other animals. There continues to be no evidence of "intelligent" species changing positions in the natural order of things and certainly no other social animals with morals. Some species have social structure but not morality. Who decides that man-eating tigers demonstrate unacceptable behavior? Rabbits do not seek to destroy the wolves that eat them. Why should humans? There seems to be logical deficiency here that insists that humans have the right to oppose the cosmic process for the sake of our comfort and convenience. Huxley implies that we oppose the cosmic process in order to survive, but no other creatures do this. What makes us think we should or ought?

The concept of "fittest" is enigmatic, more of a circular argument. The fittest survive, so which animals are fittest? The ones who survive? "We know that many varieties of domestic animals, as well as plants, have arisen under the guiding and indeed forcing hand of man, but they are only varieties, and all tend to revert as soon as man's influence or power over them is removed."[9] We really have no evidence for the system: no intermediate states, no transitional forms, no observable changes of a species directly into another totally different one. Dawkins and Ridley suggest that the entire evolutionary process is gene-controlled rather than species-controlled. Ridley contends that "we are far more dependent on other members of our species than any other ape or monkey. We are more like ants or termites that live as slaves to their societies. We define virtue almost exclusively as pro-social behavior, and vice as anti-social behavior. The conventional wisdom in the social sciences is that human nature is simply an imprint of an individual's background and experience. But our cultures are not random collections of arbitrary habits. They are canalized expressions of

---

9. Migeod, *Aspects of Evolution*, 18.

our instincts. That is why the same themes crop up in all cultures—themes such as family, ritual, bargain, love, hierarchy, friendship, jealousy, group loyalty, and superstition. Instincts, in a species like the human one, are immutable genetic programs; they are predispositions to learn."[10]

Ridley quotes Dawkins that "we are survival machines—robot vehicles blindly programmed to preserve the selfish molecules known as genes. Given that genes are the replicating currency of natural selection, it is an inevitable, algorithmic certainty that genes which cause behavior that enhances the survival of such genes must thrive at the expense of genes that do not."[11] Dawkins has called the genes "selfish" and that they create *memes*, or units of cultural information transferable from one mind to another. The human gene then lives in a host (humans) and powerfully transmits information to the host that will facilitate the survival of the gene. For Dawkins, "evolution depended not on the particularly chemical basis of genetics but only on the existence of a self-replicating unit of transmission— . . . the gene." So then, the gene replicates itself and transmits the cultural information from itself to the next human host, thus propagating or developing an inheriting understanding of culture, like morality and religion. The major problem for Dawkins' idea has recently appeared in genomic research. The gene, in fact, only stores or contains information but does nothing with it. Other molecular elements and forces actually "move" the information.[12] Dawkins had assigned a sentient-like quality to genes, which implies intelligence or plan—hardly a random, purposeless situation. Now we know that here are so many other factors involved in the transmitting of DNA information and that genes are simply "encyclopedias" or containers of information. Other forces must use the data, and Dawkins' idea has no foundation in evidence.

Stewart explains that

---

10. Ridley, *Origins of Virtue*, 6.
11. Ridley, *Origins of Virtue*, 18–19.
12. Meyer, *Signature in Cell*, 453–80.

Enigmatic If Not Ineffable

> some secrets lie deeper than the genetic code. Genes are fundamental to earthly life but their role in determining form and behavior tends to be overstated—especially in the media. Genes are not like engineering blueprints: they are more like recipes in a cookbook. They tell us what ingredients to use, in what quantities, and in what order—but they do not provide a complete accurate plan of the final result . . . In trying to understand life, however, it is SO tempting just to look at life's recipe book—its DNA code sequences. DNA is neat and tidy; organisms are messy. DNA can be captured by little more than a list of symbols; the laws of physics require sophisticated mathematics even to state them . . . As a consequence, we are in danger of losing sight of an important fact: there is more to life than genes. That is, life operates within the rich texture of the physical universe and its deep laws, patterns, forms, structures, processes, and systems . . . DNA is not the secret of life . . . It is an essential secret, but not the only one.[13]

Huxley defined "fittest" as "the best, and best means moral." Not all evolutionists hold to this idea that fittest is only most moral. Some admit that Darwin's idea was more inclined to the necessities of physical survival, and conclude that human intelligence afforded people new ways to adapt to environment and competition from other species for food, shelter, and protection from harm. The film *2001*, based on Arthur C. Clarke's book of the same title, illustrates this view as one scene shows the ape-man learning to strike one bone upon another and realizing the strategic effect of such use in driving away enemy competitors at the water hole. So, "fittest" depends on conditions. Thus men must define the evolution of ethics as dependent on developing conditions of society.[14]

E.O. Wilson and several other scholars have sought to explain the social evolutionary development of morals in the study of sociobiology. The idea is that genes play a decisive role in human behavior to improve fitness for survival, which results in social

---

13. Stewart, *Life's Other Secret*, x–xii.
14. Huxley, "Evolution and Ethics," 236.

processes conducive to their continued existence. The individual is not as important to the population as its genes. Homogenous groups have common genes which, when passed along to the next generation, will result in behaviors that will be more likely lead to survival.[15] The problems with this idea are similar to Dawkins' idea of the selfish gene. We have discovered that genes are not the driving force. Genes do not transmit any information, but other molecular elements are the chief factors in the use of the data stored in genes. Therefore, social conventions and traditions are not so much transmitted by impersonal genes, but by personal values of persons. Even in animals, there are some which protect young and some which do not. Both kinds of offspring have survived, so no pattern of sociobiology can be derived from this example. There is no evidence that species which have become extinct did so because their genes did not transmit survival behaviors, nor any evidence that the survivors' genes did. Instincts are much more complex behaviors than gene-driven information for which genes can claim responsibility. As Card explains,

> "Jane isn't rational either," said Miro. "She's just like us. Just like the Hive Queen. Because she's alive. Computers, now, those are rational. You feed them data, they reach only the conclusions that can be derived from the data— but that means they are perpetually helpless victims of whatever information and programs we feed into them [not unlike the idea of selfish genes or the inevitable cosmic process]. We are living sentient beings, we are not slaves to the data we receive. The environment floods us with information, our genes give us certain impulses, but we don't always act on that information, we don't always obey our inborn needs. We make leaps. We know what can't be known and then spend our lives seeking to justify that knowledge."[16]

Huxley believed in what he called "sound ethical principles," which reflect actions that are contrary to the "lower nature" of humanity

---

15. https://en.wikipedia.org/wiki/Sociobiology.
16. Card, *Children of Mind*, 113.

exhibited by the "passions," the desires for selfish aggrandizement and mistreatment of others. "The science of ethics professes to furnish us with a reasoned rule of life; to tell us what is right action and why it is so." Ape and tiger methods of the struggle for existence are not reconcilable with sound ethical principles.[17] The problem of evil has demonstrated itself as a major problem that humans must overcome; evolution is "full of wonder" and beauty, but also pain.[18] In Hinduism and Buddhism, evil is an illusion. "There is nothing good nor bad but thinking makes it so." The cosmos is good, man escapes evil by destroying our human "fountain of desire whence our vices flow," i.e., asceticism, enlightenment, selflessness.[19]

The Stoics saw that "the cosmic nature is no school of virtue but the headquarters of the enemy of ethical nature." Man has a lower nature, the animal, which leads to savagery. Man also has a higher nature, reason, which leads to virtue.[20] Modern thought is fresh, though the human mind is much like it was twenty-six centuries ago.[21] "Modern speculative optimism, with its perfectibility of the species, [promises the possibility of] the reign of peace."[22]

"The majority of us are neither pessimists nor optimists." Good or evil [is] "affected by human action," essentially [most] all believe "evil can be diminished," by training our intellects and energies.[23] Hastings contends that instincts "are the fundamental impulses of nutrition and sex, which Wundt contends, men and animals alike possess 'to form the inalienable foundation of human society as well as of animal association.'"[24] Moral concepts

---

17. Huxley, "Evolution and Ethics," 224.
18. Huxley, "Evolution and Ethics," 224.
19. Huxley, "Evolution and Ethics," 228–31.
20. Huxley, "Evolution and Ethics," 232–33.
21. Huxley, "Evolution and Ethics," 234.
22. Huxley, "Evolution and Ethics," 234.
23. Huxley, "Evolution and Ethics," 235.
24. Hastings, *Encyclopedia of Religion*, 129.

T.H. Huxley's Problem with the Cosmic Process

have their basis in feeling, not in reason";[25] mutual aid is the key; "morality has arisen because it is socially useful;[26] the social animal must be altruistic if the herd is to survive; its tendencies towards self-regardfulness are restrained by communal action whose one end is the common weal."[27] Problems arise with Hastings' notion in that, first, there is no evidence from nature. Generally, social herd animals will not sacrifice their own lives for the sake of their young or the elderly of their group. Normal behavior for them is to run, and protect themselves primarily. Secondly, what part does instinct play in herd behavior, rather than conscious altruism? From our study of "social" animals, instinct and perhaps some intelligence (as in primates or dolphins) dominates their behaviors, but none of these "intelligent" animals will sacrifice its own life to save another of the group. Altruism appears to be only a human characteristic.

Isaacs "suggested that morality emerged as a parameter of animal behavior as a consequence of the conflict between gregarious and predacious motivations. Man became the 'ethical animal' because of his biological dependence upon social organization and human morality is essentially a rationally formulated code of behavior which must exist between members of a community if that community is to survive."[28] But ants, bats, monkeys, etc., did not become ethical—though they obviously have biological dependence upon social organization. Why didn't they develop morality? Not all codes are rationally based nor based on what one group considers rational, such as Geneva in the Reformation, monastic orders, Islam, cannibalistic tribes, and a host of others.

Bertrand Russell believed that

> other moral rules, such as the prohibitions of murder and theft, have a more obvious social utility, and survive the decay of the primitive theological systems with which they were originally associated. But as men grow

---

25. Hastings, *Encyclopedia of Religion*, 624.
26. Hastings, *Encyclopedia of Religion*, 624.
27. Hastings, *Encyclopedia of Religion*, 625.
28. Isaacs, *Survival of God*, 182–83.

Enigmatic If Not Ineffable

more reflective there is a tendency to lay less stress on rules and more on states of mind . . . All the great mystics . . . what they value is a state of mind, out of which, as they hold, right conduct must ensue; rules seem to them external, and insufficiently adaptable to circumstances.[29] Some cultures have valued what Western society calls murder and theft, i.e. American Indians, South American tribes, Nazis, etc. Also "primitive" is a prejudiced word, assuming a cultural, technological inferiority, as well as a certain lack of a "civilizing" factor. Such categories are not only prejudicial but assume that certain cultures (Western) have evolved at a higher level and serve as the example for all other cultural values. Russell makes a good comment on state of mind, if he means that which within emerges as "character," a personal rather than societal behavior.

Penrose asserts that "the issue of 'responsibility' raises deep philosophical questions concerning the ultimate causes of our behavior. It might well be argued that each of our actions is ultimately determined by our inheritance and by our environment—or else by those numerous chance factors that continually affect our lives . . . is there actually something else—a 'self' lying beyond all such influences—which exerts a control over our actions? The legal issue of 'responsibility' seems to imply that there is indeed, within each one of us, some kind of an independent 'self' with its own responsibilities—and by implication, rights—whose actions are not attributable to inheritance, environment, or chance."[30] As an example, Westaway suggests that

> all authorities concur in maintaining, for example, that it is wrong to commit murder. But one philosopher tells us that it is wrong because it is inconsistent with the happiness of mankind, another tells us that it is wrong because it is contrary to the dictates of conscience, a third because it is against the commandments of God, a fourth because it leads to the gallows. Now how are we to

---

29. Russell, *Religion and Science*, 224.
30. Penrose, *Shadows of Mind*, 36.

account for this curious mixture ... the strange variety exhibited in ... these various systems ... ? Why does not as great a divergence manifest itself in the results arrived at as we undoubtedly find the methods employed? Indeed, why are there not as great a variety in the criminal actions themselves? Why isn't murder condoned in some philosophies, as it has in some cultures? As well, this understanding that there is the idea of good and bad, only in humans, causes some consternation with evolutionary development, as does the fact that the variety suggest choice rather than purely convenience or practicality. If the process is effective and morality makes a species more fit to survive, why the lack of consistency in value? And yet why the consistency that there is such a thing as morality?[31]

Huxley, though an adherent of evolution, considered the cosmic process inadequate to provide sufficient abilities for human to act morally. He insisted that the moral and immoral sentiments have both naturally developed. "The thief and the murderer follow nature just as much as the philanthropist."[32] But such natural development now needs adjustment. "Cosmic evolution may teach us how the good and the evil tendencies of man may have come about, but, in itself, it is incompetent to furnish any better reason why what we call good is preferable to what we call evil than we had before ... but all the understanding in the world will neither increase nor diminish the force of the intuition that this is beautiful and that is ugly."[33] It is a fallacy that evolution advanced biologically and "men as ethical beings must yield to the same process to help them towards perfection."[34] Clearly, for Huxley, evolution did not resolve the issue of human animal behavior, the problem of evil. All Richard Dawkins would support was protection of so-called scientific truth from deliberate libel against it.[35] "At present,

31. Westaway, *Science in Dock*, 5.
32. Huxley, "Evolution and Ethics," 235.
33. Huxley, "Evolution and Ethics, 235.
34. Huxley, "Evolution and Ethics," 235.
35. Dawkins, *Devil's Chaplain*, 40–42.

Enigmatic If Not Ineffable

we get away with our flagrant specieism because the evolutionary intermediates between us and chimpanzees are all extinct."[36] That's a huge assumption based on no fact. Dawkins is pro-life, but not pro-human life. Specieism assumes human life is the most valuable species of life.[37]

Gribbin asks the important question. "If the universe was 'born' and is changing and will die, how can evolution be an improvement? Or a development?[38] Milton echoes Gribbin's concern that the cosmic process, if such a prominent actor in the drama of life, should be able to account for what we see or expect to see in the world. "Do we really believe that black people are black by accident? What kind of accident was it? Why don't we see such accidents happening today? Why does the fossil record not show us such accidents happening in the past? . . . if we don't see genetic mutations—the accidents of inheritance—because they are very rare, then how can there have been enough of them to produce anything as complex as humans?"[39] That question may answer Gribbin's important issue. The cosmic process cannot be seen to be at work today. Huxley's concern that the weakness of the cosmic process actually seems to counter his support of it. The evidence of a continual "process" appears to be lacking.

Jones equates Darwinian evolution with variation, "change within species on the domesticated level, i.e. pigeon to pouter to runt to turbit, but these are still birds." Here, genetic changes required a mind, a design, of a human being to achieve. There is no evidence brought forth to demonstrate pigeon to reptile.[40] "Natural variation, the raw material of evolutionary change."[41] But this can't be demonstrated; no transitional forms exist, no modern observation has demonstrated a complete macro-evolutionary change. Biological classification is arbitrary anyway—from Aristotle: some

36. Dawkins, *Devil's Chaplain*, 135.
37. Dawkins, *Devil's Chaplain*, 135.
38. Gribbin, *Omega Point*, 7.
39. Milton, *Facts of Life*, 10.
40. Jones, *Almost Like a Whale*, 28–51.
41. Jones, *Almost Like a Whale*, 55.

human being must recognize relationships, even to assume that, such as panda to raccoon (now no longer recognized by 2009). Genes are the way to categorize, as Jones does on page 59, but even then the groupings are arbitrarily decided. "We may agree that all species of living things can do for themselves all that is necessary for their preservation, and can adapt themselves to circumstances. Some can do it better than others; but there comes a time when all their efforts are unavailing and the species either perishes or only a small remnant survives, perhaps by reason of some modification, down to a later period."[42]

Perhaps it is simply a perception problem, as Gullberg suggests in a discussion of mathematics. "There is no such thing as only one unassailable, mathematically true, geometry. From a mathematical viewpoint, any geometry—or any other branch of mathematics—that does not produce contradictions is acceptable. Another matter of concern is, however, to find the geometry that gives the most accurate representation of the physical world."[43] Indeed, an accurate representation of the physical world should be the goal of all science. But all systems and theories to date have failed in one way or another to give the whole picture. Hence the continued search for the ultimate element from which all things are made. That science seems to have proposed to have achieved the absolutes of reality has not enjoyed the popular approval in the twenty-first century that appeared to be so in the earl twentieth. Howard revealed that "many people no longer trust modernity. People still believe but not want to belong to institutions. They distrust authority (even scientific authority) as a source of truth. They want a more personalized intuitive approach."[44] Modernity did not "work" for postmodern thinkers. Problems exist for them that modern science cannot resolve, as they perceived to be promised in the twentieth century. Societies seem to be less societal and more individual. Ethics must be efficacious or at least applicable

---

42. Migeod, *Aspects of Evolution*, 16.
43. Gullberg, *Mathematics*, 384.
44. Howard, *Shopping for God*, 273.

for everyone, in spite of the narcissistic philosophy prominent in so many postmodern perspectives.

Huxley's hope was that the deficiencies of the evolutionary process could be overcome by the efforts of humanity. Science through reason has the power to loft humanity above the animal nature and develop temperate and benevolent societies. "The history of civilization details the steps by which men have succeeded in building up an artificial world within the cosmos. Huxley recognized that societies and their governments have laws to resist the 'natural' aspects of human behavior. In every family, in every polity that has been established, the cosmic process in man has been restrained, and otherwise modified by law and custom. Further, Huxley considered science and art to have been the vehicles for this constructed superiority over evil actions. The organized and highly developed sciences and arts of the present day have endowed man with a command over the course of non-human nature greater that that once attributed to the magicians."[45] "The point is that knowledge in general and science in particular does not consist of abstract but of manmade ideas, all the way from its beginnings to its modern and idiosyncratic models. Therefore the underlying concepts that unlock nature must be shown to arise early and in the simplest cultures of man from his basic and specific faculties. And the development of science which joins them in more and more complex conjunctions must be seen to be equally human: discoveries are made by men, not merely minds, so that they are alive and charged with individuality."[46] "Science has no methods for deciding what is ethical."[47] Russell also perceived the same perspective, "the fact that science has nothing to say about 'values.' This I admit."[48]

Carl Hempel accepts that "to explain the phenomena of the physical world is one of the primary objectives of the natural sciences . . . the purpose of science, which after all, is concerned to

45. Huxley, "Evolution and Ethics," 237.
46. Bronowski, *Ascent of Man*, 13–14.
47. Dawkins, *Devil's Chaplain*, 39.
48. Russell, *Religion and Science*, 223.

develop a conception of the world that has a clear, logical bearing on our experience and is thus capable of objective test. Scientific explanations must, for this reason, meet two systematic requirements, which will be called the requirement of explanatory relevance and the requirement of testability."[49] Toulmin's critique allows that "certainly, every statement in a science should conceivably be capable of being called in question, and of being shown empirically to be unjustified; for only so can the science be saved from dogmatism."[50] "Now and then there may have to be second thoughts about matters which had been thought to be settled, but when this happens, and the lower courses have to be altered, the superstructure has to be knocked down too, and a batch of concepts in terms of which the scientist's working problems used to be stated—'phlogiston' and the like—will be swept into the pages of history books."[51] "If we interpret the idea of 'the uniformity of nature' in this particular way, the only question is, whether we should not replace it entirely by the idea of the uniformity of scientific procedures. Perhaps we ought."[52]

Huxley declares evolution the enemy of morality, that evolution promotes the animal nature of humans, and cannot resolve the problem of evil naturally.

a. The theory of evolution encourages no hope for the solution of "curbing the instincts of savagery in civilized men."

b. Only the developed intelligence of men can "change the nature of man himself."

c. We have "emerged from the heroic childhood of our race" and now must "strive in one faith towards one hope," our hearts "set on diminishing it" [evil in society].[53]

---

49. Hempel, *Philosophy of Natural Science*, 47–48.
50. Toulmin, *Philosophy of Science*, 81.
51. Toulmin, *Philosophy of Science*, 81.
52. Toulmin, *Philosophy of Science*, 154.
53. Huxley, "Evolution and Ethics," 238.

Enigmatic If Not Ineffable

If humans propose to overcome evil and selfishness in society, evolution must be restrained and restricted. "Social progress means a checking of the cosmic process at every step and the substitution for it of another, which may be called the ethical process; the end of which is not the survival of those who happen to be the fittest, but of those who are ethically the best. Ethically best is the practice that involves a course of conduct which, in all respects, is opposed to that which leads to success in the cosmic struggle for existence."

   a. "In place of ruthless self-assertion it demands self-restraint;
   b. In place of . . . treading down all competitors, it requires that the individual shall not merely respect but shall help his fellows;
   c. It repudiates the gladiatorial theory of existence."[54]

The existence of laws and our human sense of morality indicates that we have been trying in history to resist evolution. "Laws and moral precepts are directed to the end of curbing the cosmic process, reminding the individual of his duty to the community, to the protection and influence of which he owes, if not existence itself, at the least the life of something better than a brutal savage."[55] "Neglect of these considerations attempts to apply the analogy of cosmic nature [evolution] to society, a misapplication of the stoical injunction to follow nature; the duties of the individual to the state are forgotten and his tendencies to self-assertion are dignified by the name of rights."[56]

As a secondary point, Huxley even doubts the explanation of evolution that had been given at the time. Perhaps something had been left out or ignored or misunderstood. "If that which I have insisted upon is true; if the cosmic process has no sort of relation to moral ends; if the imitation of it by man is inconsistent

---

54. Huxley, "Evolution and Ethics," 236.
55. Huxley, "Evolution and Ethics," 236.
56. Huxley, "Evolution and Ethics," 237.

with the first principles of ethics; what becomes of this surprising theory?"[57]

Still, Huxley believes that evolution marches on its way, and cannot be stopped, insomuch as the earth has a certain ultimate destiny. He does not appear to be one of the philosophers who held to an eternal universe idea, which does Huxley credit, since Einstein and the Big Bang, later in scientific history, demonstrated that indeed the universe had a beginning and an expected end. "The theory of evolution encourages no millennial anticipations. If, for millions of years, our globe has taken the upward road, yet, sometime, the summit will be reached and the downward route will be commenced." Human intelligence and ability cannot stop this progression.[58]

"Moreover, the cosmic nature born with us and, to a large extent, necessary for our maintenance, is the outcome of millions of years of severe training, and it would be folly to imagine that a few centuries will suffice to subdue its masterfulness to purely ethical ends. Ethical nature may count upon having to reckon with a tenacious and powerful enemy as long as the world lasts."[59]

Huxley therefore calls for the best efforts of humanity despite the evolutionary opposition, or we shall continue to be afflicted with social evil and needless human suffering. His main point of the entire essay then is that "the ethical progress of society depends, not on imitating the cosmic process, still less in running away from it, but in combating it."[60]

Huxley's optimism reflects his confidence that humans can succeed in this war on evolution. "But on the other hand, I see no limit to the extent to which intelligence and will, guided by sound principles of investigation, and organized in common effort, may modify the conditions of existence, for a period longer than that now covered by history. And much may be done to change the

---

57. Huxley, "Evolution and Ethics," 237.
58. Huxley, "Evolution and Ethics," 238.
59. Huxley, "Evolution and Ethics," 238.
60. Huxley, "Evolution and Ethics," 237.

Enigmatic If Not Ineffable

nature of man himself." It "ought to be able to do something towards curbing the instincts of savagery in civilized men."[61]

To critique Huxley's views, five issues need to be considered:

1. The cosmic process as an explanation of the origin and development of life may not be valid.
2. Survival of the fittest may not be a valid explanation of the behavior of humans.
3. Objective moral principles may not be the result of human evolutionary development.
4. The cosmic process as a theory of development of life may indeed have weaknesses.
5. The cosmic process may not be amendable by any natural force.

There are several logical problems that could arise in considering the notion of evolution of species based on natural selection and the survival of the fittest.

The first issue that arises is the instinct to survive itself. Why does any species have an instinct for survival? What made survival the driving force of life? We assume that survival is a desire, drive, or force that pushes the species to compete for resources, but that drive appears to be inclusive of all species. It is conceivable and logical to conclude that a random process would not necessarily produce such an attitude or instinct in every species of living things. Life could have been simply the fact of existence without "drives." We assume instincts for such because that's what we think we see in the natural order.

Another major problem is death. If an impersonal, physical/chemical force can create life, why would it also create death? Death is not logically a necessary corollary to life produced by a random, purposeless natural process. As well, why doesn't this life-creating force continue to create life today? Evolution cannot answer these objections satisfactorily.

---

61. Huxley, "Evolution and Ethics," 238.

Secondly, we also assume that this drive to survive includes aggressive competition for life resources. But why would competition be a force in random selection rather than something else? Wouldn't life itself, very existence, be sufficient as a result of evolution? Logically, if a force of some kind brought life into nonliving matter, the very fact of existence would satisfy the theoretical necessity. The things that then lived would simply live and then die; even with a desire to survive, the species could have simply adapted to eat whatever was there, including such things as air and water. Why would it be necessary that food for animals be species specific, if the life developed randomly, without order or purpose? Logically, there would have to have been some pre-existing force that required evolution to move in such a definitive direction.

Third, what made animals compete? What makes one species "fight" another for existence of that species? What is there about the cosmic process that requires aggression? We assume aggression, fighting, and ruthless conflict to be natural yet if species evolved randomly, logic dictates that some other means could have appeared such as sharing, moving from one location to another when scarcity came, or simply dying without struggle. How would one species "know" to kill and eat another one for the first time? We conjecture that a randomly created being would also not know purpose, i.e., to survive, to compete, to reproduce. To simply assume that the random process would build these "instincts" into the beings is a large presupposition that implies purpose.

Why is there violence in the cosmic process? The whole idea of carnivorousness can also be questioned. Some species eat plants and yet some eat other animals. There is no imperative in evolutionary theory that requires eating of flesh. If life is assumed to have been at first single-celled and then gradually multi-celled, there does not seem to be an absolute notion that violent conflict would have been necessary. How would it be better, more advantageous, and therefore fitter, for an animal to eat other animals than to eat plants? If all life came from ocean water, we could just as well assume that life would survive on ocean elements and chemical nutrients.

Enigmatic If Not Ineffable

Fourth, another problem is reproduction. The notion of reproduction itself is not required logically for life to have existed by chemical means. The chemical/energy process itself could have simply made more beings. In fact, that idea is more logical and less complicated than a competing environment that involves a complex system of species competition. The idea of sexuality and gender does not appear to be the logical outcome of chemical creation of life. Even complex beings could just as well have multiplied like the simple celled animals, by cellular division.

Fifth, there is in the cosmic process the assumed notion that animals seem to care that they survive. Otherwise there is no reason for an instinct for survival to develop. We look at the natural order and, because we care about our own existence, we superimpose on the animals and plants a desire, or a force, that makes them try to survive. We see them fight and kill and we assume it is for survival sake, but that could also be simply the way they are. They fight and kill because that is their nature or that they do those things without purpose other than to eat or protect themselves, just because that is the nature of life. We so like to personify our own values and thoughts then project them on the animal world when life may just be, by nature, violent and heartless. Natural randomness doesn't answer these questions. Random purposeless pointless life logically doesn't lead to competition and the purpose of perpetuating and the need to exist. How would it know that survival was the greatest value? How would it know self-interest and to compete, kill, or defeat another "competitor"? We're assuming a built-in drive to survive but there is no evidence or logic to convince that the drive must be there at all. I think we can call into question the description of evolution as defined by Darwin that requires complex processes when simple ones would have done just as well for life to exist. What we see in the animal and plant world does not necessarily reflect a logical picture of a chemically based, purposeless, random selection of life.

Many evolutionary theorists, including Huxley, attribute man's success of survival to organization, though there are other species who also organize yet without the development that leads to superior species. Huxley as well decries the process by which man has succeeded by claiming that it has or will let us down now that we claim to be civilized. Huxley rejects the cosmic process as the future hope, assuming that we now know better than the principle upon which all life process and human development heretofore has depended for millions of years. What are these conditions, especially since they appear to change? Utilitarian? That has been rejected since Nazism. No evolutionary progress? That idea seemed to be destroyed by the 1920s and the Great War.

Evolutionary geneticist H. Allen Orr says that "we haven't a shred of evidence that morality did or did not evolve by natural selection."[62] Pearcey maintains that "The force of sheer logic became clear a few years ago when a book came out called *The Natural History of Rape*. The authors made the disturbing claim that rape is not a pathology, biologically speaking, but is an evolutionary adaptation for maximizing reproductive success . . . the 'product of the human evolutionary heritage.'"[63] Such a conclusion would support Huxley's claim that the cosmic process must be overcome, but clearly indicates that the cosmic process itself did not develop the notion of morality.

So if evolution changes, or man changes the essential nature of evolutionary changes or results, it will become something other than fittest or natural selection; the force of change will become the will of man. Is that not contrary to the cosmic process? Will that not change the whole destiny and process of development in the universe? Is that not immoral in itself?

Huxley should have considered some distinct theoretical possibilities:

1. Evolution may not be the enemy of man's ethical nature.
2. Checking the cosmic process may not result in social progress.
3. Laws and moral principles may not curb the cosmic process.

---

62. Pearcy, "Darwin Meets Berenstain Bears," 56.
63. Pearcy, "Darwin Meets Berenstain Bears," 56, 59.

Enigmatic If Not Ineffable

"And if nature can produce such rich diversity as the present animal and plant kingdoms by pure chance, why is it that thousands of years of serious guided selection by mankind has resulted only in trivial sub-specific variation of domestic plants and animals, while not one new species has been created?"[64] "Watch a bird building a nest. Is the bird methodical? Undoubtedly. Is it working according to a plan? Apparently. Then is it intelligent? Hardly, for it is simply repeating exactly what innumerable generations of its ancestors have done before. Its method never varies. It is customary to say that the bird is acting in accordance with instinct, but what is instinct? We do not know, though people who use the term seem to suggest that instinct is something inherited."[65] "That within their own province scientific methods are perfectly sound cannot be denied. But those methods are quite useless in any exploration of human actions or human motives, except in their primary demand for bed-rock facts."[66] "Ask any half dozen intelligent friends to write down definitions of the common terms truth, goodness, beauty. The differences will be amazing... beauty may be thought of subjectively or objectively. There will be no agreement about the true essence of any one of them. And here scientific method can give no help."[67] "Needless to say, humanists are evolutionists believing that the future evolution of this planet rests in our own hands. To guide us in this task, and also in our personal life, humanists teach that we need values. And where do these values come from? Well, according to the British Humanist Association's introduction to humanism called the Humanist Perspective, these values were 'discovered during evolution' and 'such values include telling the truth, being honest, accepting responsibility, playing fair, cooperation for the common good, and caring for others.' One wonders whether the author of this paper has ever heard of evolutionary concepts such as 'the survival of the fittest' or 'the selfish

---

64. Milton, *Facts of Life*, 11.
65. Westaway, *Science in Dock*, 33.
66. Westaway, *Science in Dock*, 50.
67. Westaway, *Science in Dock*, 50.

gene!'"⁶⁸ "Now the theory of evolution teaches that human beings are the product of chance natural processes without the intervention of any supernatural agent. Furthermore, some argue that if we are just animals, the result of random natural processes, then why should abortion, or even euthanasia, be considered wrong? Putting to death an unwanted puppy or kitten is not considered immoral, so why is it wrong for an unwanted unborn child . . . or an old sick person?"⁶⁹

Finally, we consider critically Huxley's conclusion.

Evolution's progress toward its ultimate goal cannot be stopped. This is an assumption of downwardness; thus evolution will eventually be destructive, i.e., the Big Implosion. There is nothing anyone can do to stop this. Why would evolutionists care to stop it or to live differently now than what is supposedly destined for all life? Yet they do care; they insist on morality of some kind, particularly protection of themselves from crime and war. But if morality doesn't really mean anything for selfish survival, why would anyone object to a culture that wants to survive more than other cultures? Why isn't it acceptable for a totalitarian regime to conquer the world and oppress the "weaker" people groups if that makes them the "fittest"? So said Nietzsche in the nineteenth century. It's wrong because deep inside every person has the awareness that people are not just animals on the food chain and we all have some sense of morality, a God-given capacity, an innate recognition of right and wrong. John Gribbin, PhD, science journalist, BBC, writes "That puzzle is brought home with full force by the light of the sun in the daytime. This represents an imbalance in the universe, a situation in which there is a local deviation from equilibrium. It is a fundamental feature of the world that things tend towards equilibrium."⁷⁰

> No one, so far as I know, has ever claimed to have seen a species created. Neither has anyone seen a species

---

68. White, *Wonderfully Made*, 14.
69. White, *Wonderfully Made*, 15.
70. Gribbin, *Omega Point*, 6.

evolved from other species.[71] It is significant that neither in ancient nor in modern times is there any instance of the merging of one species into another collateral species, and so on into another by means of slight gradations or variations. For instance, we see pygmy elephants alongside great elephants but there is no merging. I make this statement following a number of writers, but there is in fact no evidence whatever to show that the individual in any given species was in any way smaller in the early days of the species than it was at the time of the extinction of that species, or that there was any material difference in the species at its end from what it was at its beginning.[72] "If we consider the mineral world: there is no evolution there. Each metal or precious stone is itself and nothing else. One does not descend from another. One does not merge into the other. There was a separate and sudden appearance of each into the world, and, evidently, in many places at once. It is hard not to call this process creation."[73]

Huxley's main conclusion is that, "the ethical process of society depends not on initiating the Cosmic Process . . . but in combating it."[74] And in so doing, change the essential nature of man, that through our intelligence, "be able to do something towards curbing the instincts of savagery in civilized man,"[75] i.e., resolve the problem of evil that men perpetuate on themselves and become ethically good.

Aristotle, Greek philosopher and scientist, pupil of Plato, who was a pupil of Socrates, held that any logical argument could be reduced to two premises and a conclusion, and laid down in three basic laws, or principles, of logical reasoning, often referred to as classical logic or Aristotelian logic:

71. Migeod, *Aspects of Evolution*, 19.
72. Migeod, *Aspects of Evolution*, 19–20.
73. Migeod, *Aspects of Evolution*, 105.
74. Huxley, "Evolution and Ethics," 237.
75. Huxley, "Evolution and Ethics," 238.

1. The principle of identity. A thing is itself: A is A.
2. The principle of the excluded middle. A proposition is either true or false: either A or not A.
3. The principle of contradiction. No proposition can be both true and false: A cannot be A and not A.[76]

Huxley's argument may fall into the trap of the principle of contradiction, since he believed that the cosmic process was the force that brought life into being, directed it over time to evolve, and then tried to defend a concentrated, rational effort on the part of humans to resist the process for the sake of morality. He seems to say that, because the cosmic process logically brings pain and suffering to all life, and we do not like such pain and suffering, we should develop practices that contradict the process. So morality then becomes an accommodation to personal preferences, nearly a utilitarian goal of pleasure over pain because we can, rather than because there is some real meaning to morality. Howard says, "certainly moral absolutes seem best tempered according to the situation. Generally they should come from within, then be tested by our friends. We can only ever have partial knowledge of good and evil, but few would see genocide, paedophilia, environmental destruction, or greed as good."[77] On the contrary, good cases can be made in history where many nations and governments, with the consent of a majority of their citizens, have approved of genocide. Capitalism is built on greed, the desire to possess as many material possessions as possible, preferably more than the neighbors. Starving people have no problem destroying certain parts of the environment to use it for obtaining goods, as in some areas of rainforests. Some ancient cultures, such as in Greece and Rome, exhibited societal approval of paedophilia. Friends tend to have common goals and perspectives. "Testing" ethics on them will only get basic approvals of these goals such as in Nazism, Stalinism, Maoism, and Japanese atrocities in World War II. Situation ethics has already proven to be an undependable and unstable system

---

76. Gullberg, *Mathematics*, 216.
77. Howard, *Shopping for God*, 277.

for societies. Rules keep changing with every change in leadership or law. Postmodernists distrust modernity because science didn't resolve the basic problems of human society, as some people expected, nor provide all the desired moral results that were claimed. "Undoubtedly the most hopeful prospect for psycho-social evolution is this trend towards more compassion both in the formulation and the enforcement of moral systems. Or . . . man is slowly learning that his survival depends on his ability to use reason to encourage his sympathetic emotions, and to suppress those which are antisympathetic."[78] Social evolution is better with compassion? Is postmodernism more compassionate than modernism? We are having more conflict now because of emotions; our reason is now being used to encourage agreement and stability. Our "sympathetic" emotions result in narcissism, incoherent, incongruent, and intolerant behaviors and philosophies. Walsh concurs that science itself is greatly affected by the societal trends of the times. "Cogent reasons of intellect and scholarship have been suggested for pursuing . . . a resolution of the case . . . Compelling is one reason in particular: the rare chance afforded to learn more about the interior process of science in itself and in its relation to society. Especially relevant is a third reason, uncovering the pernicious effect on science of fashionable ideas, the degree to which a prevailing paradigm may influence and even dominate not only thinking but discovery."[79] Without a standard of morality that extends beyond the current trends of society, or is considered higher than individual emotive choices, societies are victims of merely personal preferences which can be anything.

Huxley suggested that man can change the world by repressing his savagery.

Why bother? If evolution is true and life is meaningless, who cares if man is "savage," meaning just like the animals, only "fitter"? Why does Huxley or any evolutionist feel the need to rebel against the cosmic process? Why are there ethics at all? Not for societal benefit—the natural world functions without ethics and some

78. Isaacs, *Survival of God*, 193.
79. Walsh, *Unravelling Piltdown*, xx.

T.H. Huxley's Problem with the Cosmic Process

animals are highly societal. Without ethics, life would be brutal, merciless, and vicious like the animal world (as we perceive it)—without emotion, care, love, or compassion, which we must have or life is total hell. We will not live that way. Why not? Why does that notion bother us if evolution is the norm and the natural?

Roland Howard implies a certain guilt in news and entertainment media that "the media as a meaning-making machine which idealizes wealth, romance, excitement, and immediate gratification and which shows life as a series of intense experiences seems to having an effect on virtually all forms of spirituality,"[80] not to mention paradigms of life and societal values. Huxley's relative, Julian Huxley, said that "first and foremost come the consequences of evolution and its acceptance. If man's body has evolved, then so has his mind. Our mental powers are not only relative, developed in adaptive relation to the world around us, but there is no reason whatever supposing them in any way complete."[81] But what compels one group of people to refrain from annihilating another group who is competing with them for resources, as is claimed regarding animals? Why do we have emotional compassion for others? To be sure we survive in a world of limited resources, why do we not highly value abilities and attitudes that result in dominance of one group over another. Nazism would be the most obvious philosophy to adopt, which sought to eliminate weaker groups and to enhance and perpetuate one group. Yet we clearly see a repugnance of such paradigms and seek to rid the world of such "extreme" notions. Why would anyone do that if humans' minds evolved along with their bodies? We should see more and more effect ways to use our minds to eliminate competitors.

For, in the main, social morality relies upon the exploitation of reason and the subjugation of emotion. In theory, therefore, such a system should reflect the best interests of the majority. The purely secular society therefore suffers from the disadvantage that it has to sacrifice an undue proportion of individual freedom in order to impose its legislation. This will be so no matter how sensibly

---

80. Howard, *Shopping for God*, 272.
81. Huxley, "Evolution and Ethics," 59.

Enigmatic If Not Ineffable

it has tried to arrange for the suppression of greed in the common good. These secular societies, therefore, are always in danger of becoming police states.[82] But, in evolutionary terms, why wouldn't a police state be satisfactory if that would bring about the proper survival of the fittest? Minorities, by definition, are fewer and therefore weaker and more likely to be the groups that will not survive. We clearly see that such a philosophy is intolerable but are reluctant to blame evolutionary ideas, as Huxley does, for promoting the survival of the fittest in human society. Penrose agrees that "as we open our newspapers or watch our television screens, we seem to be continually assaulted by the fruits of Mankind's stupidity [warfare, unrest, violence, conflict, squandered prosperity]. Though we believe ourselves to represent the pinnacle of intelligence in the animal kingdom, this intelligence seems sadly inadequate to handle many of the problems that our own society continues to confront us with. Thus, not only does our technology provide us with an enormous expansion of the scope of our physical selves, but it also expands our mental capabilities by greatly improving upon our abilities to perform many routine tasks. What about mental tasks that are not routine—tasks that require genuine intelligence?"[83] What is "genuine intelligence"? Is intelligence the key to unlocking the highest values of evolution—survival? If it is, then the *use* of intelligence should be highly significant, beyond gathering food, selecting the strongest mates, or finding ways to protect ourselves. Intelligence must include more than cleverness or technological inventiveness but must as well be comprised of a lack of Penrose's concern with stupidity and more of Isaac's emotive values. Could this concern be defined as sensibility, the reasonable awareness that all people have value beyond the survival of the fittest? If so, we must define intelligence as anti-Cosmic Process, as Huxley has done.

Teilhard insisted that "for some two hundred thousand years or more, we agreed, mankind as a whole has not ceased to advance in the direction of higher cerebralisation and closer socialization.

---

82. Isaacs, *Survival of God*, 188–89.
83. Penrose, *Shadows of the Mind*, 8–9.

Human brains have reached the limit of anthropogenesis but the areas still open are collective cerebralisation or socialization. Forces are making us more in common. In the case of man, therefore, collectivization, super-socialisation, can only mean super-personalisation; in other words it ultimately means (since only the forces of love have the property of personalizing by uniting) sympathy and unanimity. It is in the direction and in the form of a single 'heart' that we must look for our picture of super-mankind, rather than in that of a single brain."[84] Teilhard assumes that the emotional quotient is the ultimate evolution and that socialization depends on the emotive unity of humanity. These conditions have yet to be demonstrated in society. Rather, forces like religiosity, politics, economics, and ideology have made more significant inroads into social development, which cannot be called development in any real sense. Human societies have not improved the human condition much, even with technology. We still have an inclination to cruelty and self-destruction. The super-socialization of our collective "heart" seems more remote every year. Yet our non-unity has not been aimed at a complete recognition of survival of the fittest, rather a survival of the clever, the selfish, the best funded, whether intelligent or not, from Penrose's definition. We are more segmented rather than globally similar and divided rather than united. Teilhard also assumes that a "single heart" is more highly evolved than the "'single brain" and reason is inferior to emotion in evolutionary survival terms, though historically and even today, there is no such paradigm.

Finally, we must come to some conclusions too. Kluger refutes the notion that sociobiology or genes control us with his study of the brain. "Specialized neurons are being found [in the brain] that allow us to mirror the behavior of people around us, helping us learn such primal skills as walking and eating as well as how to become social, ethical beings."[85] Gorman adds to the contradiction of sociobiology that "the underlying principle remains. When too many of the rules change, when what used to work doesn't

---

84. Teilhard, *Science and Christ*, 157–60.
85. Kluger, "New Map of Brain," 39.

anymore, your ability to reason takes a hit. Just being aware of your nervous system's built-in bias toward learned helplessness in the face of unrelieved stress can help you identify and develop healthy habits that will buffer at least some of the load."[86] There has been no evidence that genetic information, intent on survival, adjust to changing "rules" such that the previous information can be altered to fit new situations.

Pinker's notion is that science, locating sentience in the brain, will destroy the social idea of soul, separate from physical brain, which will then eliminate our belief that we are free agents responsible for our choices.[87] For all our efforts to that end in the study of the brain, postmodern society has turned against such a "scientific" notion and focused even more on the passions of the soul as the "real" locus of person. Pinker's utopian empathy that all people will exhibit when distinctions and differences are removed fails to consider the importance of the non-physical in humanity from which we draw our notions of ethics and morality. Wright confirms this idea. "We like to think our views on right and wrong are rational . . . but ultimately they are grounded in emotion."[88]

Clearly, even evolutionists like Huxley sensed the rightness of morality, law and order in society, protection of children, peace in community with other persons, protection of property, and freedom. Evolution, according to Darwin, was heartless, mechanical, and meaningless. Huxley and others of his persuasion recognized that life must have meaning and must have other senses than survival. Evolution did not, and does not, provide the necessary explanations for these logical problems.

---

86. Gorman, "Six Lessons," 59.
87. Pinker, "Mystery of Consciousness."
88. Wright, "How We Make."

2

The Foundation of Morality
Is Morality Subjective or Objective?

MORALITY MUST BE OBJECTIVELY derived because

1. the concepts of good and morality exist;
2. cultures differ regarding certain moral actions, thus there is the need to discover which is right, but cultures are similar regarding the existence of and need for morality;
3. relativism is not logical and does not work,
4. for moral principles to be legitimate and consistent, they must be derived external to human societies. Otherwise morality is merely one person's choice or feeling, not an understanding of truth;
5. of the existence of religion.

People recognize a moral aspect to the worship of deity; even if the deity does not exist, we still perceive a need for morality to be decreed by Someone or something greater than humanity.

First, the concepts of good and morality exist. The very existence of the idea of good argues for something in human society that is different than the bunnies and the wolves. "Nature" is

Enigmatic If Not Ineffable

amoral; the bunnies do not protest the fact that wolves eat them. There is no notion, outside of Bambi, that the animals consider some of themselves good and some bad. Thus, the nature of humanity is somehow different than other creatures. Somehow we know that certain principles and actions are "good" and acceptable, rather than simply necessary for existence. We contemplate the abstract thought of moral principle itself, and the universality of such an idea. All human cultures do not have exactly the same moral codes, but all cultures have a moral code. This concept of the nature of humanity argues for a code of morality that fits all people; we seek it, we believe it, we feel that we need it.

Second, cultures differ regarding certain moral actions, but all cultures recognize similarly that morality exists. Human cultures do not always value the same moral actions. One culture may value theft, as in some of the American Indian tribes of the plains, particularly against enemies. Such action showed bravery and skill in battle. Another culture might abhor the idea that one person should be allowed to steal from another, and the value here is the sanctity of private property, as in the Western industrial countries. When differences occur, the question arises as to what moral idea produces the right action. Somewhere in the history of human cultural interaction, these two values will collide. They cannot both be right. What is the truly moral idea? Hence there is a need for an objective criterion, again one that transcends either culture, rather than simply be a preference of one culture over another.

Human cultures do tend to agree about some moral ideas, such as murder of one's own people, cruelty (except against enemies), rape, and other violent actions which force one person's will upon another. The fact that there is agreement seems to indicate a common source of moral conscience, a standard to which all humans attempt to adhere. C.S. Lewis called this idea the "Moral Law" or a natural law of morality,[1] an idea similar to Immanuel Kant's "Law of Nature" idea. Kant grounds his concept in an *a priori*, purely practical human reason, which Lewis identifies in the *imago Dei* within human nature. Kant's categorical imperative

---

1. Lewis, *Mere Christianity*, 21–26.

The Foundation of Morality

insists that morality is based on valid impersonal principles, in the intrinsic worth of right itself, upon which humans should act. "To duty every other motive must give place, because duty is the condition of a will good in itself, whose worth transcends everything."[2] These principles acted upon rationally would then bring harmony and order to human social interaction. Any fully rational person would necessarily recognize the good and act according to the imperatives.[3] Kant insists that the point of morality is the principle not the frailty or inconsistencies of human nature.[4]

The conflict between the Protagorean Sophists and Plato points out the ancient history of the subjective-objective battle. The Protagorean notion, advocated by modern scholars such as Ruth Benedict, Melville Herskovits, Sir Edward Tylor, and others,[5] was that ethics are simply convention, since different societies behave in different ways. "Although some conventions may be more effective than others, what matters most is not their precise content but the fact that they are shared and adhered to."[6] The logical effect of such an idea, however, emerged quickly, i.e., that one can challenge any or all conventions and propose casting away all restraints, individual egoism, and the moral survival of the fittest. Gautier's notion that it is in the "enlightened self-interest" of the egoist to cooperate with society and act morally[7] belies the problems, first of the source of an egoist self-control to cooperate with values he doesn't accept, and second of the possible existence of an absolute moral value.

Other thinkers, such as Glaucon in Plato's *Republic*, then suggest that society requires some kind of conventions in order to function.[8] But this notion requires the awareness that humans must have some kind of restraints or we will likely destroy

---

2. Kant, *Foundations of Metaphysics*, 20.
3. Kant, *Foundations of Metaphysics*, 20.
4. Kant, *Foundations of Metaphysics*, 24–25.
5. Satris, *Taking Sides*, 2–22.
6. Norman, *Moral Philosophers*, 7.
7. Beauchamp, *Philosophical Ethics*, 50–53.
8. Norman, *Moral Philosophers*, 13.

Enigmatic If Not Ineffable

ourselves. Why is this so? Social Darwinism proposes that humans are like all animals, and the strongest achieve their personal ends. Might makes right. If this notion were the case, humans would not be aware of ideas like equality, fairness, discrimination, injustice, oppression, and the like. We would just live or die, like the bunnies and the wolves, because that's just the way things are. No one would propose alternatives. Some Eastern thinkers believe that chaotic moral behavior results from disharmony in the functioning of the universe. But what makes a person violate the harmony? What forces create disharmony that makes one malfunction? The Christian philosophical answer is that human sin is the problem, the reason people act to harm themselves and others. God's laws provide the constraint that allows societies to function and good to happen in the world.

Richard Taylor believes that people can be "good" without God, or any divinely-given external standard. He indicates that people know "there are reasons for not stealing, there are reasons for not assaulting, there are reasons for not lying. These things hurt people."[9] However, if there is no standard, why does pain matter? Bunnies suffer pain when eaten, but that's just the way things are in nature. If there is no umbrella of moral standard, why do we not just accept that the strongest, "fittest," will survive, whether by force or guile or whatever is necessary? Just because someone hurts does not make an action immoral. The same logic applies to Taylor's contention that morality is mere convention, neither natural nor supernatural.[10] When in Rome, do as the Romans. One support Taylor uses to bolster his argument is Aristotle's assumption that people can discern right from wrong. But that notion sounds more like Lewis' description of the moral law, built into humans from a divine source, rather than support for cultural convention.

Again, Taylor points to the "ancient Greeks" for support of moral convention by saying that ethics has a natural basis: human need, i.e., things we all have and need for security, safety, love, etc. But from where do these recognized needs come? Who says they

---

9. Craig and Taylor, "Is the Basis?"
10. Craig and Taylor, "Is the Basis?"

are needs, rather than preferences? Without an external standard that directs our attention to what is good and evil, what actions humans should expect from each other, and what rules should be used in society to restrict evil behavior, we have nothing consistent to appeal to. Hitler cannot be condemned if his cultural convention dictates annihilation of Jews, if we only appeal to one human's or one culture's choice over another's. Who's to say that one group's convention is better or worse than another's, and upon what basis can we say it? Taylor says "all you need is to be human"; one doesn't need a morality revealed by deity to treat other people right. This perspective supports a holocaust. Historically, we have not seen human beings respond as Taylor expects. We have been brutal, cruel, vicious, and destructive regardless of our creeds, conventions, or customs.

William Craig believes that naturalism does not provide a sound basis for morality. "If naturalism is true, objective right and wrong do not exist,"[11] to which Taylor agreed. As well, Craig says that without God, there is no objective right or wrong. If naturalism is right, then we cannot condemn war, oppression, or crime. Some actions may not be socially advantageous, but cannot be called crime or wrong. Craig argues that Taylor, and naturalism, define morality as social skill, but such skill can develop cruelty as well as kindness. With Taylor's naturalism, "no one is morally obliged to be virtuous." Nietzsche's Ubermann defines his own virtue but becomes self-centered, elitist, and cold-hearted, which Taylor condemns.[12] Plato's philosopher-king reflects a similar non-egalitarian preference for one type of human over another. Equality of worth and value of life do not logically emerge from naturalism, for humans or bunnies.

Third, relativism is not logical and does not work. Subjective morality adheres to or can be defined as relativistic ethics.[13] Relativism, on the surface, sounds attractive to many people, especially Western culture because of our traditional value of individualism.

11. Craig and Taylor, "Is the Basis?"
12. Craig and Taylor, "Is the Basis?"
13. Johnson, "Antipodes."

Enigmatic If Not Ineffable

Make your own way; take care of number one; pull yourself up by your own bootstraps. There are many aphorisms to be found in Western literature that promote the supremacy of the individual. Thus when one philosophy promulgates a morality of personal choices, a smorgasbord of opportunities, individualism rejoices. Relativistic morality allows that each person make his/her own choices of behaviors, based on what the person believes to be best for him/her. Do what you like, or what feels good to you. There is no external authority to dictate one's behavior. But "relativism contradicts the law of non-contradiction where two opposites cannot both be true."[14] Truth essentially functions, by definition, as the excluder of the false. "Each truth claim excludes any claims that are contradictory to it," and therefore one view, say the Christian theist view that morality is God-given and absolute, is no more "narrow" than its opposite: the atheist's view that there is no God.[15]

On the one hand, there are external authorities that dictate some behavior, such as the system of laws in a country, enforced by police and courts. If relativism is true, then why the need for authorities at all? Won't people, out of their natural goodness and recognition of the freedoms and needs of others, withhold destructive behaviors for the sake of the society? That has never been the historical case. Well then, we need the authorities only for those actions that hurt people. Why? Pure relativism can have no such restriction. And even if it does need restrictions, why select the ones we do? How does a society identify innocence or guilt? What would be "wrong" with eliminating groups of people who bring emotional, economic, or political pain to the rest of the culture? Why do we call it persecution or oppression rather than necessary cultural cleansing or protective elimination?

On the other hand, relativism does not work. Somewhere in the course of human affairs, people who have chosen conflicting values will collide. Who, then, gets to behave the way they want to? There must be some resolution which, without discriminating laws or authorities, can only lead to "might makes right." A

---

14. Geisler, *Baker's Encyclopedia*, 238.
15. Geisler, *Baker's Encyclopedia*, 238.

The Foundation of Morality

Nietzschean superman, the one with the power, gets his/her way. Perhaps even the majority will get the right. In any case, it cannot be that everyone will be able to choose his/her own way of living. There will always be restrictions, conflicts, authorities, something that allows one mode of behavior and restricts another mode. "The idea of values being subjective is a denial of the need or possibility of morality. Since morality is subjective, and right and wrong are not real, it makes no sense to judge others . . . [thus] justice is impossible."[16]

Fourth, legitimate moral principles must be derived external to human preference. The consequences of subjective morality are destructive to a society and individuals. Values become subjectively determined based primarily on feelings and desires. "It means there is no such thing as good or evil . . . it is not, and cannot be, a statement about reality."[17] As some thinkers assign morality to cultural conventionality and insist that all cultures' codes be tolerated or respected, a question arises. Though differing cultures exercise various moral behaviors, are there any which function relatively? The answer is negative and the argument is specious. Just because societies differ does not mean that there is no absolute moral value. One cannot combine several different moral systems into one completely relative one. Each of the different societies has one system, none of them have a relative one. This may seem a pragmatic response, but the fact implies the question of the existence of absolute moral values. Logically then, moral relativism fails. "Subjectivism seems to boil down to anarchistic individualism, and conventionalism fails to deal adequately with the problems of the reformer, the question of defining a culture, and the whole enterprise of moral criticism."[18]

Plato, however, is one of the strong supporters of objective morality (see Book 6: *The Republic*). The eternal forms are not changeable; a fixed external standard applies to everyone.[19]

16. Landauer and Rowlands, "Subjective Value."
17. Landauer and Rowlands, "Subjective Value."
18. Satris, *Taking Sides*, 22.
19. Kim, "Moral Realism."

Enigmatic If Not Ineffable

Aquinas' morality is "grounded in principles that are fixed in nature . . . discernible through reason" and were planted in nature by God as a reflection of his character and being. "All human laws are judged in reference to these."[20] Some scholars think that, in naturalism, emotions are simply motivators connected with the needs of the being, and these needs provoke the emotions, and thus the being acts.[21] All is well and good if we think only humans are involved, but the bunnies have no such motivators, and why would humans have them if we are simply advanced beings in the food chain? Christian ethics, as well as most religious philosophies, recognizes the "reality of moral virtues," as well as the mandate that humans should be morally virtuous according to an objective, external pattern.

No one person can be sure that his personal preference of morals is the correct one. In fact, no humanly-derived system of morality can be certain of truth and right. We do tend to make errors in judgment and discernment. The charge that transcendence can interact with material need not, indeed cannot, be explained in empirical terms if such an interaction has occurred is arbitrary. But non-explanation does not mean the contact hasn't been made. The force which motivates the objectivist is that truth and right must be done; the transcendent standard commands and requires it, whether there be sanctions against those who disobey or rewards for the obedient. Human nature recognizes a need to be moral and good; if the standard points the way and insists by its very existence that humans are bound by its tenets, then resistance to the standard brings negative sanctions whereas obedience produces social and personal well-being. Kant declares that "unless we wish to deny all truth to the concept of morality and renounce its application to any possible object, we cannot refuse to admit that the law of this concept [reason which determines *a priori* the will to duty] is of such broad significance that it . . . must be valid with

20. Kim, "Moral Realism."
21. Thagard, "Ethical Coherence."

The Foundation of Morality

absolute necessity and not merely under contingent conditions and with exceptions."[22]

Kant's ideas criticize the subjectivists concerns about limitations and restrictions of an objective standard by indicating that such concerns reveal the "imperfectly rational being," one who only feels constrained by commands which are necessary manifestations of the principles rather than imposition on an unwilling being who can individually decide which actions they should take.[23] Kant declares that truth and right do exist objectively.

Finally, the very existence of religion provokes a strong argument for the existence of objective morality. Why would humans "invent" such religious notions? Simply because natural events, such as storms, or natural objects, like the sun or moon, exist and have influence on earthly life? Humans recognize that there is something, or someone, more powerful, bigger, and eternal that exerts control over human life. If there was no such recognition, there would be no reason to do anything but seek shelter in storms and perhaps feel the heat of the sun. Why would one environmental element be considered more important than another? Yet human seems constrained to worship something, to submit to greater power, to conceive of an eternal, supernatural being, and conceive of this being in certain ways. "The belief that morality requires God is not limited to theists, however. Many atheists subscribe to it as well."[24] Besides the conception, we have exhibited similar notions of how this being must be approached, satisfied, and obeyed. The ideas of living after death, the necessity for redemption or absolution of personal sin, sacrifice, and prayer would be wholly unnecessary and unthinkable if humans lived like bunnies and wolves, like naturalism implies. Somehow we practice religion because somehow we know there is something or someone else, greater than we, to whom we owe allegiance and obedience. It is not enough to say that we simply wonder how we came to be and invented deity to meet our needs for meaning. Why would we even

22. Kant, *Foundations of Metaphysics*, 24.
23. Paton, *Moral Law*, 24–31.
24. Schick, "Morality Requires God."

Enigmatic If Not Ineffable

recognize such a need? How is it that we have sentience at all, beyond the kind animals possess?

Plato asserted the objectivity of values through his notions of the forms.[25] Goodness itself exists in distinction to good things.[26] Goodness is perfect, while our good actions change and are not consistently good, or perceived as good. But the idea, the form, of good persists in our knowledge and awareness. Christian philosophy identifies this inherent knowledge with the *imago Dei*, the built-in recognition of the essential goodness of God. Cudworth, one of Cambridge's Platonists, asserted that "human minds contain the imprint of Divine wisdom and knowledge."[27] The strongest arguments then, the ones which provide the most logical and practicable aspects, conclude that human common sense and experience recognize the existence and superiority of the idea of objective morality over the weaknesses of subjectivism.

---

25. https://www.reasonablefaith.org/videos/debates/craig-vs.-harris-notre-dame/.

26. Norman, *Moral Philosophers*, 23.

27. Hutton, "Cambridge Platonists."

3

Xenophanes' Concept of God

XENOPHANES OF THE LATE sixth and early fifth centuries BC should be credited, in opposition to his critics and misinterpreters, with an advanced contribution to the Western philosophy of religion, namely that there is one God. First, he exposes the weaknesses of the Greek pantheon. Then he satirically demonstrates the narcissistic limitations of human conceptions of the nature of the divine. Third, he logically structures a coherent concept of the nature of the only God. Finally, he reveals how his concept explains certain observable natural phenomena in an account of physical reality.

1. Xenophanes said, "there is one god, among gods and men the greatest,"[1] but why would that idea be unusual for his culture, in its history? He explains that everyone in his culture had been taught by the famous poets and writers, including Homer, that a pantheon of multiple deities existed and affected the lives of humans in various ways. The nature of these gods, however, defies the whole notion of deity. Anaximander had earlier conceived of the underlying "stuff" of the universe as *apeiron*, an unexplainable something. But Xenophanes carries the notion much further by attacking the mythology of his time and giving definition to the ineffable source of life. The famous writers "attributed to the gods

---

1. Freeman, *Ancilla*, 23.

all things that are shameful and a reproach among mankind: theft, adultery, and mutual deception."[2] Illogically also, humans thought that gods were born and had clothing, voices, and bodies as well.[3] Surely, gods had to be more than glorified albeit often more immoral than humans, by the definition of "god."

It appears that Xenophanes viewed God from two perspectives. First, the Homeric gods demonstrated behavior that simply resembled the behavior of humans. God, by definition, had to be someone greater, better than humans in some way(s). He said that the one God is "greatest among the gods, not like mortals in form or thought." Thus worship of this God implies that an all-encompassing greatness is a factor of worship, which means primarily submission to and reverence for a being greater than oneself. As well, morality seems to be recognized by all cultures in some form or another, but reveals a certain weakness or propensity in humans to behave badly at times, as opposed to behaving well at times. There is an inherent recognition that there are good and bad actions and God is "not like mortals in form or thought." Hence he must be better morally as well as greater in power. Moral goodness then becomes another criterion for worship.

2. Xenophanes indicated that humans are basically narcissistic and limited, making God in our own images. "Ethiopians have gods with snub noses and black hair, Thracians have gods with grey eyes and red hair,"[4] and even animals, if they could draw, would draw gods that look like themselves. Finite, limited, contingent beings tend to conceive of gods like us; thus gods had become finite and limited, again contrary to a higher and clearer view of what a god is. By attacking the anthropomorphic ideas of deity, Xenophanes developed an idea that found "fertile ground two centuries later in Aristotle, and a millennia later in the theology of St. Thomas Aquinas. The idea was that the underlying substrata [of reality] is not a substance, or a material; it was pure causation."[5]

2. Freeman, *Ancilla*, 22.
3. Freeman, *Ancilla*, 22.
4. Freeman, *Ancilla*, 22.
5. Provost, "Xenophanes," https://web.archive.org/web/20030529042259/

The concept of *imago Dei* is usually considered in a broader sense than mere specific physical appearances. The concept includes reason, emotion, spirituality, sense of morality, laughter, music, and other attributes unavailable to animals. There is, however, something to be said that human beings look the way we do because, somehow, we do resemble God. The term "image of God" first appears in Genesis 1:26 and 27 as "image" and "likeness," which clearly implies appearance. The very same phrase, "image and likeness" appears in Genesis 5:3: "And Adam lived a hundred and thirty years, and begat a son *in his own likeness, after his image.*" Again, the phrase clearly indicates a being that resembles its sire. Xenophanes' concern was that humans thought of gods as just another type of creatures like us, only immortal. He recognized that many people make God in their images, which for Xenophanes is a big mistake. This anthropomorphic view of God tends to do what Xenophanes opposed and brings the notion of deity down from heaven, as it were, to the human level of relative powerlessness and immorality. A more balanced view which credits Xenophanes' transcendent God, as well as recognizes that humans do have some kind of a broad relationship with our Creator, would be strongest.

3. God is the same as the one; he is the only deity, not like these imagined gods of the pantheon, nor like humans in body or mind. "He sees as a whole, thinks as a whole, and hears as a whole. And he always remains in the same place, not moving at all, nor is it fitting for him to change his position at different times."[6] Xenophanes defines god in majesty, omnipresence, and transcendence, a being able to interact with the universe, similar to definitions from Hebrew, Christian, Zoroastrian, and Islamic theologies. Indeed, Xenophanes did travel in his life to many places in the Mediterranean world and intentionally studied various religious ideas.[7] Perhaps contact with broader notions of deity added to his insight. "In fact, in his inconceivable power and infinite intellect, about which one cannot possibly jest, let alone deride, Xenophanes' god

---

http://n4bz.org/gsr/gsr6.htm.

6. Freeman, *Ancilla*, 23.

7. Freeman, *Pre-Socratic*, 88–89.

seems more like the later Judeo-Christian god than the human-like Homeric gods."[8]

The God of Xenophanes is like the Judeo-Christian God in several ways. First is the concept that God is greater than any other being. Second, that God is not begotten or created from something or someone else, thus he has always existed. Third, that though the Judeo-Christian God "speaks" (revelation) to his people, the anthropomorphic descriptions of him are not really adequate to account for his nature. Fourth, he is one. Fifth, he is omniscient (all sight, all hearing, all thought). Sixth, God creates or acts "by the thought of His mind." Seventh, he is immutable.

4. Finally, Xenophanes indicates that motion, the notion of change in Greek thought, is initiated by God, "without toil . . . by the thought of his mind."[9] The omnipotence of God, the capacity to create with only his mind, also mirrors other theologies, but, more importantly for Greek thought, reveals a role for divinity in the explanation of the physical universe and anticipates Aristotle's unmoved mover. "God for Xenophanes has the modality for affectivity; from his thoughts actions occur."[10] Motion and change, so visible in the physical universe, are results of the unchanging god who affects how things act in the world we see.

Xenophanes may have viewed the "gods" that he mentions like several other religious groups in the world, either as manifestations of the one (Hinduism) or as lesser spirits that influence human life at times (American Indian religion or Shintoism). These kinds of lesser spirits exert some power greater than humans but are, of course, not the one true God. Xenophanes could have also believed that the notion of "gods," though faulty and false, was a frame of reference for the discussion of the one God with the culture of his day. A similar phrase is used in Exodus 15 in the Song of Moses, "Who is like unto thee, O LORD, among the gods?" (Exod 15:11). The song addresses Hebrews who had resided in a strongly

---

8. https://web.archive.org/web/20003043017165 6/www.ablemedia.com/ctcweb/showcase/deyoung4.html.

9. Freeman, *Ancilla*, 23.

10. Semogas and Dhaliwal, "Xenophanes."

polytheistic Egyptian culture, and the reference to "gods" likely refers to these Egyptian gods which were condemned and bested by Jehovah in the famous plagues of Egypt (Exod 7–12).

There have been some who criticize the idea that Xenophanes' concept is monotheistic or even legitimate. Aristotle thought that Xenophanes was not clear and not a thinker of physical sciences.[11] Following Aristotle, Theophrastus "attributes to Xenophanes the view that Being is One, but admits that Xenophanes' views do not really belong to a record of scientific and metaphysical inquiry."[12] Aristotle, I think, valued scientific thought along the lines of his own observational, material theories and had little patience with metaphysical, mystical ideas. That seems clear with Theophrastus' admission that Xenophanes' thought was not aimed at scientific inquiries. That does not mean, however, that the poet, the artist, the dreamer may not perceive the revelation of an ultimate power or being who affects all of the universe. Empirical knowledge is but one of the many ways humans "know" things.

Owens, to Xenophanes' statement that there is one god, greatest among the gods, said that "this is hardly the utterance of one who today could be called a monotheist. It praises a god who is the greatest among a plurality of gods, a sort of *primus inter pares*. As it stands, it need be nothing more than the rhapsodist's hymn to a Zeus purged of Homeric anthropomorphism."[13] Owens neglects the logic of Xenophanes' statement since the one God is greater than men and gods, hence he is greater than the concept of multiple deities and men alike.

Armstrong described Xenophanes as "a wandering religious teacher rather than a philosopher . . . who attacked the traditional mythology and preached a sort of pan-animism; God for him is one, acting as a whole, immovable, governing all things by the power of his thought, and (as far as we can tell from the fragments of X which survive) an immanent all-pervading world-soul."[14]

---

11. Guthrie, *History of Greek Philosophy*, 368–69.
12. Freeman, *Pre-Socratic*, 93.
13. Owens, *History*, 23.
14. Armstrong, *Introduction*, 12.

Enigmatic If Not Ineffable

However, there is nothing in Xenophanes' statements that suggests a world-soul idea. God is called by the personal pronouns "him" and "he"; he is a being who thinks, sees, and hears as well as sets things in motion by thought, thus interacting with the universe for change; he remains in one place and does not change. The world-soul idea would require the deity to change with the universe, act with the universe, and exist because of the universe; this is not in Xenophanes. Guthrie agrees that pantheism in Xenophanes has been sufficiently denied by other scholars on several grounds. First, Xenophanes' concept focuses on the unity of God in himself, not in the world, and also that a God without change cannot be part of a changeable universe.[15]

Some think Xenophanes was inconsistent in his concept of deity since he mentions in one fragment that men who enjoy themselves should "first of all praise God with decent stories and pure words," but then they should "always to have respect for the gods, that is good." Kroner said, "In spite of his criticism, he [Xenophanes] also paid homage to the gods of the national religion, as his word demonstrates: 'It is good always to pay careful respect to the gods.' But he especially blamed Homer and Hesiod for having 'ascribed to the gods all things that are a shame and disgrace among men.'"[16] Concern here is for context, since Xenophanes was best known for his satirical wit. The context of his views in poems or satires may not give us a straightforward philosophical view every time. As well, his long life of nearly one hundred years might make his views differ over time.

In contrast to the unworthy polytheistic deities who behaved poorly, even by human standards, exhibiting deception, adultery, theft, and the like, came Xenophanes' monotheism. Through the eyes and words of an itinerant poet/performer emerged a vision of the universe that was broader and more comprehensive than those of previous philosophers of natural science. Xenophanes does a credible job to describe the possibility of the existence of only one deity, given most of his contemporaries' awareness of

---

15. Guthrie, *History of Greek Philosophy*, 381.
16. Kroner, *Speculation*, 62.

Xenophanes' Concept of God

the weaknesses of the pantheon. He provides in his view of the unmoved transcendent deity a "rational and coherent" explanation which positively accounts for the role of the divine and the spiritual. Just the very notion of the "greatest and best" and its application to the concept of deities brings an inevitable identification of a single best. As well, Xenophanes posits only one God like this, unlike humans or finite immortals. From the nature of God's power, Xenophanes argues for one God, emphasizing the characteristic of holiness, a quality not possessed by the members of the pantheon. Something in humans, which biblical theologians identify as part of the *imago Dei*, allows us to recognize morality, the very notions of good and evil, and the desire, even demand, for purity and holiness in God.

The concept of greatness, according to Xenophanes, means God is greater than any being or combination of beings, who act inconsistently or incongruently. God must be one to act in an unlimited way. Hence as in Hebrew theology, the LORD is one; there is no other, Xenophanes' one God provides an explanation for the creation of the universe, the existence of laws and morality, and the great benevolence bestowed by God on people in time and history. Kroner agrees that "Xenophanes did not yet announce the God of Genesis, but he had an intuition of the oneness and spirituality of the biblical Creator."[17] The polytheists' conception of the gods brought nothing like Xenophanes' argument nor any sufficient explanation for what common observation and personal intuition recognizes as a vital aspect of life: the religious urge. God's power also directly implied his eternal existence since nothing greater could have created him, and thus he always was, and is, one. Aristotle said that "Xenophanes, who was the originator of this attempt to reduce things to a One . . . gave no clear account . . . but directing his gaze to the whole heavens he says that God and the One are identical."[18]

---

17. Kroner, *Speculation*, 61.
18. Freeman, *Pre-Socratic*, 93.

4

Seneca and Virtue

IN LUCIUS SENECA, ROMAN Stoicism receives its most recognized expression, particularly in his ethical philosophy. Seneca's argument that virtues are derived from nature, necessarily as part of human nature, fails to consider several other issues of metaphysics and ethics. While his view may explain why humans recognize the notion of virtue and can do good things, Seneca's concept ultimately lacks complete satisfaction for several reasons.

Seneca's view consists of two basic parts. First, there is an all-pervasive, all-encompassing providence that governs the universe. An orderly universe could not exist nor persist without a caretaker (providence). This providence is deity. This world, then, is the best of all possible worlds. Second, the providence (God) determines what is good. God guards and protects the universe from true evil and its tendency to total destruction. Good is found within humans. Whatever happens is supposed to happen and is best for humans.

Seneca concludes therefore that happiness is not the goal of life but virtue, the sense and nature of which is implanted in the very nature of humanity by providence. Adversity and ill-fortune are simple exercises to strengthen human virtue. Disaster is virtue's opportunity. Events and conditions of life do not matter, rather our response to them: how we bear difficulties. A soft easy life weakens human character.

A materialist could counter Seneca's view that if there is no providence, events are simple predictable effects of various causes. One who believes in the possibility of deity would also respond that if humans are not basically good, there must be a need for an intervening providence. But what kind of providence? The most important aspects of life point to possible accountability to a deity. The evolutionist could claim that if the universe is all there is and ever has been, then what may come in progress is unknown and unpredictable.

How does one measure a good person? If bad things happen, do we know whether the person is being punished, trained in virtue, or simply affected by an imperfect natural order? Is this indeed the best of all possible worlds? If the biblical explanation is true, a better world seems to have existed before the disobedience of Adam and Eve (Gen 1) and a better one will be created at the end of time (Rev 21:1–8, 22–22:5). If the evolutionary view is true, how would anyone know if a better world once existed or will exist in the future? If the materialist view is true, this is the only possible world that has always existed; "better" is irrelevant and impossible.

Seneca might reply to the materialist that if there is no providence, there is no order, thus no prediction of effects and no science, and any sense or logic to the way the universe is. To the spiritualist he might agree that the deity should have some power over human beings, based on how each person responds to the exigencies of life. Is the person's life full of honor and dignity or debasement and dishonor? Seneca clearly values peace over strife, since what is, should be. The evolutionist makes Seneca's point for him exactly: that providence made the world in such a way that anything that develops will be good. All events are good, realized only by the one who responds properly. The natural order is perfect for humans. Even if we were in a different world, we would still have to base our virtue on how well we responded to events, in a Stoic way, of course. This is the best world for humans, or providence would have made it differently.

The strengths of Seneca's view are first, an awareness of a natural order that comes from somewhere or something. This is similar to the classical argument from design, which has gained strong support recently among some postmodern scientists.

Second, there is an awareness of the nature of goodness in providence, hence the human recognition that there are such notions as "good" and "evil." Third, Seneca's ethic provides a coping mechanism, with historical evidence for general success, for human life, particularly for those people who experience hardships. Fourth, Seneca provides a positive perspective about human life and promotes building stronger aspects of human character such as courage, humility, nobility, and virtue. Finally, moral integrity, virtue rather than emotional satisfaction, is the goal of life.

As well, there are weaknesses in Seneca's view. The innate goodness of humans is problematic. There is no recognition of possible offense to a deity; the very concept of a divine state of holiness apart from human virtue seems ignored. Seneca does not satisfactorily explain the nature of evil in the universe. He seems not to answer the notion of a once better world or better future world. Seneca does not delineate particular notions of what effects are bad or good and whether actions could be different depending on social law, crime, and punishment.

On the whole, Seneca's Stoicism is a powerful social response to the vagaries of human life. It is a positive attitude, character-building, and being trustful of divine will which was easily adapted by religious persons in later times.

5

The Case Against Science

SCIENCE HAS BECOME AN unreliable epistemological resource for several reasons. First, the assumptions of science are suspect. Second, the scientific method exhibits narrow limits to the acquisition of universal knowledge. Third, the conclusions of the scientific community at large are questionable and inadequate. Fourth, the practice of science has developed a particular perspective about its place in the world of knowledge that diminishes all other avenues of knowledge, to its detriment. Finally, the practice of science involves a philosophical approach which makes scientism and "pure science" hard to differentiate. Thus, science itself, as an epistemological discipline, has been discovered to be unworthy of the extreme admiration granted it by the present technology-loving world.

1. The assumptions of science are suspect.

Historically and philosophically, empiricism has been shown to have clear limitations, since many persons recognize that reality consists of things which can be known through the human senses as well as things which are not known by them. In fact, the very foundational assumptions of science are suspect. Markos indicates that "many of the givens we take for granted (most notably, that the foundation of all true knowledge is material, empirical, and quantifiable) are as recent as they are unproven."[1] There also appear statements that seem to indicate that scientific assumptions should not be challenged. "No one would today think to ask why the interior angles of a Euclidian triangle sum to precisely 180 degrees. The question is closed because the answer is necessary."[2] The answer may be necessary, but perhaps is not true—perhaps it is only a convention for the use of the tool, perhaps only an arbitrary designation. Clearly, the notion can be challenged.

2. The scientific method exhibits narrow limits to the acquisition of universal knowledge.

"The basic principle, the starting point of all science, is the idea that the universe can be studied by observation and experiment."[3] Does this statement limit itself to the physical aspects of the universe? Can't the non-physical be studied by observation and experiment? The whole point of the use of senses is to employ them in the study of our existence in the universe, which includes non-physical phenomena. Even the effort to "experiment" can be done with human experience, such as in psychology, para-psychology, religious experience, and even normative religious testimony, such as the countless millions of people who testify to the same result when converted to religion. The so-called "scientific method," which appears objectively effective, has not been so practiced. The limitations of this method make it, from the very start, subjective.

Consider the aspects of the scientific method. First is the recognition of a problem or issue. These issues are not always universally acknowledged. The researcher, the scientist, must recognize the issue which requires a human decision, a human perception, that all humans may not so perceive. Then the researcher thinks of a hypothesis to resolve the problem. These hypotheses depend on the philosophical presuppositions and perspectives which the researcher brings to the research. The presuppositions follow logic

1. Markos, "Myth Matters."
2. Berlinski, "God, Man."
3. Trefil and Hazen, *Sciences*, 7.

trees, branches of thought flow which, when diagrammed, look like tree branches. At each fork in the branch, when one line of thought proceeds in one direction and another line in a different path, the philosophy of the researcher, not just the gathered data or accumulation of information, provokes the direction of thought. The next step, the gathering of more data, also depends on the direction of the hypothesis which is structured by the researcher. Then the choice of experiment and how it will be done is further decided by the researcher, based on the direction of the hypothesis. Finally, the interpretation of the data and experimental information is the most arbitrary, philosophical step of all. Hence, the conclusion can be as logical and as false as Linus' Great Pumpkin, if the philosophical basis is faulty. It need not be reiterated here the massive amount of work done in the history of philosophy, begun even before Plato, to indicate that empiricism has its challengers in rationalism, existentialism, and other epistemological methodologies.

Though some insist that the testing of any hypothesis, objectively derived or not, is itself objective, all objective testing is an illusion. The acceptance of a hypothesis depends on a subjective philosophical perspective. A good example appears in history when the inquisitors looked through Galileo's telescope and saw mountains on the moon, yet refused to believe the obvious evidence. The same could be said for many scientists who, until recently, rejected the idea that the universe demonstrates the evidence of design rather than randomness in its origin. We *know* some things without systematizing the process—love, fear, the presence of someone in the dark—when such knowledge is clearly empirical. As well, only so much data can be gathered. Even in research projects, researchers know that they must stop gathering at some point and interpret, or they will forever be gatherers. Thus, limitations of the process must be identified. Not all reality can be tested or described in "laws" that can be controlled or made predictable. Science is simply another effort on the part of humans to control and manipulate the universe, which will always be an incomplete and fallible endeavor.

Enigmatic If Not Ineffable

"[Wilson] ... provides a template that can be held up against claims to see if they belong in the realm of science. How well the template fits comes down to two questions: Is it possible to devise an experimental test? Does it make the world more predictable? If the answer to either question is no, it isn't science."[4] Then scientists should resist the temptation to prognosticate about things outside of their field. The reason this problem emerges now is that science, at least for the last few hundred years, has either attempted to achieve or been given a highly exalted status as the source of truth. At least, the scientific method has been argued as the best process, sometimes the only process that provides reliable truth. The chief philosophical problem, however, is not just the neglect of some empiricists to recognize the limitations of their methodology, but the idea that the scientific method itself is the best empirical avenue for epistemology. "We live in a world of matter and energy, forces and motions. Everything we experience in our lives takes place in an ordered universe with regular and predictable phenomena."[5] To say such a thing, to imply that only empirically obtained information is reality, is to deny all the other possibilities of knowing reality. Even in empiricism, the scientific method demonstrates weaknesses and limitations. For instance, the concept of irreducible complexity, popularized by Michael Behe, demonstrates conclusively that the world of microbiology exhibits mysteries that scientific methodology can only begin to consider. The smaller we go, the more diverse and complex the world is, and the explanation for this complexity, according to Behe, is design. This notion throws science into a quagmire of perplexity, since irreducible complexity challenges long-held Darwinian explanations for life in the universe.

We must expand our vision of possible explanations for things. We must not adopt an answer just because it is necessary to make our theories "work." Even if physicists discovered the grand scheme of a unified theory of the physical universe, we would still

---

4. Park, *Voodoo Science*, 39.
5. Trefil and Hazen, *Sciences*, 2.

The Case Against Science

not know all there is to know. The definition and methodology of scientific knowledge limits the scope.

"We learn about the universe around us by experience and observation on the one hand, and by thought and deductive reasoning on the other."[6] Is that all? Are those the only tools we have? Can there be no place for spiritual discernment, revelation, existential experience, emotion, intuition, or other non-empirical methods? Could not all these methods be combined to give us a more complete understanding about the nature of reality? We "experience" a starlit night sky. What does that word "experience" mean here? We observe the dark sky with various bright objects in it; we feel the cool, crisp night air and the quiet atmosphere brought by the repose of all life; we imagine dreams of unexplored worlds or previous pleasant nights in some other places; we sense the presence of the spiritual, unseen life all around us. These and other possible aspects of our experience cannot be totally described by the mathematical measurement of the distances to the nearest stars, or the explanation of the silver moon as merely the reflection of the light of the sun. All that is true, but reality is not only physical.

3. The conclusions of the scientific community at large are questionable and inadequate.

Thomas Kuhn declares that the power of science in the world at this time is due to the acceptance of science's paradigm. "Paradigms gain their status because they are more successful than their competitors in solving a few problems that the group of practitioners has come to recognize as acute."[7] Why are we so enamored with science? Because it "works" and we're a pragmatic, technologically-oriented culture? We're usually eager to defend science and math against all epistemological comers, such as religion, reason, intuition, and personal experience. We've given scientists the status of the ancient druid or shaman, the fountain of accuracy,

---

6. Singh, *Modern Mathematics*, 1.
7. Kuhn, *Structure of Scientific Revolutions*, 19.

Enigmatic If Not Ineffable

certainty, and authority over human society. Consider a characteristic statement found in the Time Life Science Library:

> Scientists have concluded that the one kind of message most likely to make sense to any intelligent form of life anywhere [in the universe] would be a mathematical one . . . Many of the world's great thinkers . . . have decided that mathematics represents absolute truth. In effect, the mathematicians (pure math) are saying that their work can apply to our world and universe because they designed it to apply to every possible world and universe that might be imagined along logical lines. They are saying that mathematics reaches into a realm of such ultimate sophistication that the truth or untruth of any given premise no longer matters.[8]

Though mathematics presents a viable description of our technological culture, is it not possible that, if alien intelligent life exists in another possible world, mathematics and logic might not be intelligible to them? What if the alien world is emotional, illogical (from our frame of reference), intuitive, and poetic? What if they think in completely unfamiliar patterns? It sounds like the height of arrogance to claim that we know the universal language and that we have designed a system of communication that will "apply to every possible world and universe that might be imagined along logical lines." As well, though some philosophers have claimed to be above truth and morality to their destruction and disrepute, we find that truth matters. Science and mathematics define themselves as tools for the pursuit of truth, not just mental exercise.

4. The practice of science has developed a particular perspective about its place in the world of knowing that diminishes all other avenues of knowledge.

Science is done within the paradigm selected by the scientific community, and "to desert the paradigm is to cease practicing the science it defines."[9] Indeed, the paradigm structures the very questions and problems identified by the scientific community,

8. Bergamini, *Mathematics*, 9.
9. Kuhn, *Structure of Scientific Revolutions*, 28.

The Case Against Science

which become "the only problems that the community will admit as scientific or encourage members to undertake. Other problems . . . are rejected as metaphysical, as the concern of another discipline, or sometimes as just too problematic to be worth the time."[10] The problem for modern society is that scientists often claim knowledge or authority in problems which do not really fall into the arena of scientific empiricism, such as origins of the universe, the existence of God, the purely material nature of all existence excluding spiritual existence, and others. If this wasn't enough, the massive use of metaphor in science reveals that we just don't really know as much as people think we do. Light is not a wave nor a particle; time is not a dimension; even the structure of atoms is described in terms which those elements are not. Granted, language itself requires that knowledge in all fields use metaphorical images to convey understanding. That use should tell us, though, that all fields of learning have limitations and inscrutable aspects. However, that is not the message that emerges from the public statements of scientific writers. Consider the following pronouncements from Trefil and Hazen's textbook published in 2000 for college classes in science. "Science represents our best hope to solve pressing problems" in society. Science plays a "central role" in modern society. "Our approach recognizes that science forms a seamless web of knowledge about the universe. . . . Science provides the most powerful means to discover knowledge that can help us understand and shape our world."[11]

Because the human mind is logical and reasonable, we can organize and structure entire systems of theories and ideas that "logically" flow from completely false presuppositions. Step 1, though false, leads to an inevitable logical second step, equally false, and then to other erroneous steps which lead to the false conclusion. Examples of such action are the phlogiston conclusion of science in the eighteenth century, the ether, the Great Pumpkin, Communism, phrenology, and a host of other recognizable errors in human thought. Americans have been systematically

---

10. Kuhn, *Structure of Scientific Revolutions*, 30–31.
11. Trefil and Hazen, *Sciences*, v, vii.

Enigmatic If Not Ineffable

brainwashed as a society to believe in the absolute authority of empiricism and mathematics as arbiters of all truth, simply because the results of such methodology "works" in the building of technology. That kind of pragmatic result is the demonstration of the limitations of the methodology—technology is what empiricism and math produce, but they are not the only sources of ultimate truth.

5. The practice of science involves a philosophical approach which makes scientism and "pure science" hard to differentiate.

"The central role of science education must be to give every student the ability to place important public issues such as the environment, energy, and medical advances in a scientific context."[12] Science claims to "never stop questioning the validity" of its conclusions, theories, and laws, and that "every theory and law of nature is subject to change, based on new observations."[13] Yet, science claims certain theories, such as human macro-evolution, as fact, not to be questioned, because "virtually all scientists accept" the theory as fact.[14] This kind of statement sounds like scientism, contradictory to the very definition and so-called basic principles of science itself as a field of epistemology. "Science is the systematic enterprise of gathering knowledge about the world and organizing and condensing that knowledge into testable laws and theories."[15] Must all knowledge of reality be "systematic"? There is an ultimate level of reality and human beings have access to it. Science claims to have access to this ultimate level, when in fact it does not. Not all knowledge can be systematized since other epistemological avenues such as intuition, pure reason, existentialism, and others, are valid sources of knowing reality. Science, by definition, cannot be extended to include these other arenas. Science must be limited to the empirical observation and repeated experimentation of physi-

---

12. Trefil and Hazen, *Sciences*, vi.
13. Trefil and Hazen, *Sciences*, 6.
14. Trefil and Hazen, *Sciences*, 588.
15. Park, *Voodoo Science*, 39.

cal phenomena, to determine the "how" of reality, not always the "why." Not all things can be predicted, hence another limitation of the scientific effort. We can be fooled by our observations and our judgments, but there is something real about aesthetic, religious, and emotional experience. These non-scientific experiences have been repeated by countless people for centuries, and should be considered essential for a more complete knowledge of reality.

William James' book on religious experience clearly indicates a commonality in non-empirical knowledge of people all over the world.[16] Though materialists have argued for a view of the world that includes only the reality of physical phenomena, too many people have recognized that there are other dimensions to the nature of reality. Besides James and other scholars in the psychology of religion, we include Rudolf Otto and Friedrich Schleiermacher who both delineated the existence of some being "wholly other" than humans, an existence of the reality of feeling connected to a greater existence.[17]

The issue of probability surfaces here. What evidence is necessary to make something probable? "Most of what we believe about the external world is received at second hand and rests on the prior belief that some men are more trustworthy reporters than others. The conclusion to be reached, in view of our individual mental poverty, is that we cannot avoid reliance upon some sort of authority."[18] The evidence itself must be interpreted, which again requires philosophy. If one holds to the view that there is no spiritual world or spiritual beings, then no amount of evidence will force that one to believe in miracles. "Seeing is not believing," said C.S. Lewis. "What we learn from experience depends on the kind of philosophy we bring to experience."[19] We must find the philosophy that enables us to understand our experiences and bring that perspective to the experience. Most likely, it will take all our epistemological methods, not just one, to encompass such a diverse and complex range of human experience.

16. James, *Varieties*.
17. Otto, *Idea of Holy*.
18. Trueblood, *Philosophy of Religion*, 67.
19. Lewis, *Miracles*, 3.

6

Imaginationism

IN A WORLD RECOVERING from the breakdown of logical positivism and scientism, imaginationism is the next positive philosophical approach to take. Imaginationism is the idea that the primary and most dependable avenue through which truth can be known is the imagination. Imagination means the faculty of human perception that sees things that are not as though they were. It is the faculty "by means of which we explore the order of possibility,"[1] "forming a mental concept of what is not actually present to the senses; the power which the mind has of forming concepts beyond those derived from external objects; the creative faculty" of the mind.[2] Modern Western culture de-emphasized the use of imagination as a tool for epistemology, yet every tool of knowledge acquisition, even science, has made extensive use of it. "As a faculty for combining abstracted components of experience, imagination in the privacy of thought or the intended Cartesian Theater is a useful tool for calculation and evaluation of alternative hypotheses to see where they might lead. This process makes imagination an

---

1. Martin, *Instructed Vision*, viii.
2. Little, Fowler, and Coulson, *Oxford Universal Dictionary*, 958.

Imaginationism

essential part of morally responsible deliberation and action, because of the agent's forethought."[3]

Our quest for factual and pragmatic certainty forbade that we should acknowledge imagination as a faculty that could discern reality and truth. For us, imagination was fantasy, magic, fairy tales, and superstition: the things children played with to make their unrealistic lives happy.

But modern science has failed to solve the world's problems and to answer the foundational mystifying human questions. Rationalism, empiricism, existentialism, intuitionism, and other epistemological venues seem to have exhausted their usefulness and attraction. We still seek purpose and meaning for life; we search for God and spiritual fulfillment in a multitude of ways. Emotion dominates our world and we want real roots that stabilize life and help us understand what happens and why. People in a postmodern world realize that empiricism cannot solve our human problems, but neither can science. So there emerges a more "spiritual" answer. Science is not their venue.

Postmodern people look for certain results or products from ideas and philosophies. Any acceptable notion must have "life" in it or come from it. By life, they mean force that can be felt, that charges their emotional batteries, and that can be perceived as a benefit or a pleasure. Some may say that this attitude is nothing more than an old hedonism or reworked utilitarianism. But the postmodern will say that persons not only seek pleasure but emotional reality, experience of the world, its highs and lows. People need to connect their inner beings with the rest of the universe, thus they seek spiritual and emotional sustenance, though they often really don't know exactly what that might be. They become adventurers, experimenters, not just escapists who take drugs or play virtual reality games from despair of life. Science is out of its realm in these areas. The postmodern person resists control and predictability, and is not interested in systematic anything. How will this person "know" the world? What is to be known? Only scientific and technological data and process? The postmodern

---

3. Jacquette, *Philosophy of Mind*, 155.

person defiantly cries, "No!" and seeks for other ways. To approach these issues, we must re-learn to use our imaginations, to sense and conceive the reality of our natural perceptions. Our environment is dominated by visual stimuli and now we emphasize the "picture" over the word. So imagining with insight and understanding will help us find new meaning to reality.

How would such a philosophy function to provide human connection to reality rather than fantasy? First, we recognize that imagination is an activity of the mind that can be used rationally or irrationally. Imagination is not separated from reason, rather, it is part of the human reasoning capability; "the abilities the Reason View requires most notably include the ability to see and appreciate the True and the Good."[4]

"'The historian and the literary artist,' Russell B. Nye reminds us, 'are bound by the same risks, related by the same liabilities, dependent on the same creative, imaginative powers.' The result in both instances is truth, and each version is valid within its own domain."[5] We use imagination to compose a hypothesis at the beginning of scientific inquiry. We use imagination to conceive of business opportunities or possible political solutions to social problems. In short, we use this mental power to operate in the world in a multitude of ways. Granted, we can also conceive of monsters that have never existed in physical reality. We can imagine invisible friends or dangers that have no being. So the manner, the method, by which we use imagination determines its identity as rational or irrational.

> Everything we perceive is mediated through a variety of filters—our knowledge, background, circumstances, desires, feelings, assumptions, institutional affiliations, class, status, gender, age, and so forth. We tend to see what we want to see, to remember what we are predisposed to remember. We strive to make sense of our world, to interpret as best we can. In our quest for meaning and understanding, we choose from a smorgasbord

---

4. Wolfe, *Freedom Within Reason*, 95.
5. Miller, *Laura Ingalls*, 1.

Imaginationism

of interpretants—links between signs and objects that enable us to make sense of the world we inhabit.[6]

Interpretants are interpersonal relationships in family, school, church, community, work, play, courtship, ritual, and a hundred other ways. "Meaning was not arbitrary or amenable to individual whim but was established within certain parameters by tradition, practice, authority, prescription, and common expectation."[7]

Second, we realize that imagination is limited in scope. We do not imagine what cannot relate to our experiences of reality. George Lucas, creator of the movie *Star Wars,* envisioned a multiplicity of creatures from different planets and different celestial cultures, but even the shapes and characteristics of these beings were constructed from images already known to humans. For example, the denizens of the local pub on Tatooine had heads of sharks, two human heads, pig noses, or various other appearances, but all were re-combinations of aspects of beings already known to us. We imagine with only the conceptual building blocks of experienced reality. We cannot image a being with characteristics which we have never experienced. We cannot imagine colors different from the spectrum or sounds we have never heard. "We are made necessarily ignorant of any world beyond our ideas."[8] Hence the necessity that all divine revelation had to be done in human history, with angels who appeared like people, with a human voice from God to human ears, with a written book of human language, and ultimately in the incarnation of himself in human form.

Third, since imagination can be rational or irrational, and is limited to images of reality of which we are certain in our own experiences, imagination can then be trusted to present certain realities to our perceptions. The creature may have a pig head and seal flippers in our minds, and we have not seen such a being, but pig heads and flippers are aspects of the real physical world. How do we know when our irrational imaginations are unreal? They are

---

6. Miller, *Laura Ingalls*, 70.
7. Miller, *Laura Ingalls*, 70.
8. Grave, *Scottish Philosophy*, 17.

only unreal to the extent that we do not recognize a mis-combination of real aspects and misunderstand the nature of the pictures in our heads. So it is our interpretation of imagination that qualifies our recognition of reality. "The difference between common sense and skepticism is a difference in the way of looking at the same empirical facts. For skepticism there is no right way, or if there is, nobody knows what it is. For common sense there is a right way and we know what it is."[9]

The imagination presents the real aspects; we must interpret them correctly. Hence, the importance of the philosophies we bring to the use of our imaginations. If no spiritual beings can exist in one's metaphysics, then one will not imagine the reality of such beings. Imaginary things always have some aspects of the real to them. Tolkien explains that when writers of fantasy "imagine," even to the extent of combining one set of realities with traditions of imaginary things, that confusion is not the result. The writer has created a venue to ponder the aspects of the two worlds,[10] and aspects of the real become visible in the imaginary.

---

9. Grave, *Scottish Philosophy*, 91.
10. Tolkien, *Beowulf*.

7

The Nature of Faith

FAITH IS AN ESSENTIAL aspect of religious experience. Events can often be understood by some people as aesthetic or pleasant[1] rather than religious because their frame of reference rejects the spiritual connection for a more temporal one. However, of course, there are experiences that people have that by-pass any effort on their part to explain them naturally and clearly demonstrate a spiritual situation. One British scholar described his experience, like those of many others, that convinced him of the reality of God. He had "no religion," no "real sense of personal relationship to God." He went for a walk alone one day, without particular thoughts or intentions, when he "became conscious of the presence of someone else," and realized a feeling that the "being of God" surrounded him. "It was no longer a matter of inference, it was an immediate act of spiritual . . . apprehension." The experience changed his whole perspective of the world and himself. "I had not found God because I had never looked for him. But he had found me; he had, I could not but believe, made himself personal to me."[2] The man could interpret this experience because faith had been "awakened" or become functionally directed in him.

1. Brown, *Psychology of Religion*, 90.
2. Bouquet, *Religious Experience*, 19–20.

Enigmatic If Not Ineffable

Some people, and many psychologists, deem faith to be something akin to wishful thinking. The great philosopher-psychologist William James defined faith as a "belief in something concerning which doubt is still theoretically possible"; the believer acts in faith by taking steps which are not guaranteed to turn out as he thinks they should.[3] If faith is not wishful thinking, or acting in hope that the right thing will happen, then it is non-rational self-affirmation. "Religious assertions . . . resist every objectively compelling form of rational justification, forcing believers to hold their convictions 'by faith.'"[4]

These feeble attempts to define faith fail to understand the true nature of faith, religious or otherwise. Christian (as well as most religious) faith is first built on historical fact and event, certainly comprehended rationally. These events form the logical foundation for the theological truths proclaimed which explain the meaning of the events. Therefore, doctrines are delineated and articulated based on the historical "revelation" of the nature of God and how believers of all ages have comprehended him. These are certainly not non-rational bases. The "objectively compelling form of rational justification" is no more than the scientific, naturalistic explanations of being, which depend on materialistic rather than spiritual or other justifications. There are many more truths and realities in the universe than those which science can expose.

Faith is also not merely wishful thinking. Faith is the clear, undeniable knowledge that something unseen is true.[5] Religious faith is assurance, evidence of the unseen, certainty that the spiritual world and God are what we have experienced them to be. It is certainty that what God has promised, he will do. It is rational acceptance of historical fact and prophetic promise. Any emotion connected with the exercise of faith is merely consequential or contiguous. That many Christians and other religious practitioners misunderstand the nature of faith and act as if faith is uncertain has evidently led others to define faith incorrectly. Faith is

3. Strunk, *Readings*, 196.
4. Whittaker, *Matters of Faith*, ix.
5. Hebrews 11:1.

knowing, not guessing or wishing. Why do we talk about "faith" in the context of religion and "reason" in the context of knowledge? William James' definition of faith as a species of belief "concerning which doubt is still theoretically possible" is inadequate. Faith is considered a positive knowledge, the very opposite of doubt.[6] But faith is not simply religious knowledge either, though faith has an adequate rational foundation. Faith must "make sense"; it must satisfy the rational aspect of the human experience or it will be dismissed or distrusted. Faith is rational knowledge of the unseen, based on the trustworthiness of the source of that knowledge. We have faith in human relationships because the person who is the object of our faith is trustworthy, dependable in our experience of their behavior or sentiments. We have faith that the invisible elements of the physical world exist because we observe results of their use. We have faith in historic evidence that certain persons existed and did certain things, though we have no photographs, videotapes, audio recordings, or other modern acceptable evidence to show us their lives. Faith, then, is a trust based on a reliable source or our own experience that something which we cannot see nor detect physically is nevertheless true and exists.

Whittaker represents the quintessential psychological scientist as he asserts that believers only "feel certain," and that their testimonies are unreasonable. "The most natural explanation is that we are confined to belief in matters of faith because we are not in a position to know . . . religious assertions are hypotheses—i.e. uncertain propositions whose truth or falsity might, in principle, if not in practice, be established by some kind of factual inquiry. Until we have all the facts we need, we cannot determine the truth of such beliefs."[7]

Whittaker demonstrates the weaknesses of the scientific method. He will only accept "natural" explanations of all phenomena; he will only accept "facts" which can be verified by human experimental control; he assumes all non-scientific inquiry to be irrelevant; he believes that the only valid epistemological method

---

6. James 1:5–7.
7. Whittaker, *Matters of Faith*, 3–4.

Enigmatic If Not Ineffable

is scientific; and he expects that if he personally does not have material verification, then an assertion of any kind cannot be true. Such attitudes are closed, narrow, blatantly unscientific, and ignore the great mass of phenomena for which experimental explanations cannot be obtained. We can applaud his desire for empirical assurance, but such will not be provided if he will not accept historical evidence or patterns of current experiential data in the sphere of the spiritual.

Some critics have relegated faith as certainty to "mental adolescence" in the process of human development. The very desire for spiritual knowledge, absolutes, and moral living is considered the marks of immature minds.[8] This attitude assumes that uncertainty, ambivalence, ambiguity, and relativity are characteristics of maturity. The incongruity of this argument is evident. It has been said that childlikeness is essential to faith, but not childishness or irrational adolescence.[9] There are abundant arguments that refute the notion that relativism and ambivalence are values of mature societies. If behavioral standards are merely human inventions and choices, then who is to say that one is better than another? How do we know if one human group chooses a particular set of values that that set is the best or right one? Is it simply by the choice of one human being, or even a majority in a given society? Which human should choose and who will decide? Obviously the logical extension of relativism is simply "might makes right," only those who have the power will exercise the choices.

Strunk's assertion that religious experience is simply an "attempt to break away from the dominance of the cognitive processes, and are indications that the affective have been given full sway"[10] fails to recognize as well the holistic character of religious experience. Rationality combines with affective processes to involve the entire human person in the experience. Otherwise, all emotive experiences would be ecstatic and rhapsodic, and the person would be intellectually unreachable until the episode is

---

8. Strunk, *Readings*, 158–59.
9. Matthew 18:3.
10. Strunk, *Readings*, 116.

The Nature of Faith

completed. From our normal human experiences of all kinds, not just religious, we know such not to be the case. Also, that cognition "dominates" human life is questionable. People do things for many other reasons, many of them affective, than logical.

Granted, religious experience does emphasize the awareness and importance of the affective processes of human existence, but intellectual comprehension of the experience is always ultimately essential. Without comprehension, experiences of any kind have no meaning. Bregman confirms that rational processes affirm the reality of experiences.

"Although it might be possible to mislabel an experience . . . it is not possible to overlook the occurrence of something without resorting to repression or self-deception. In the literature on inner experience, the beyond-all-doubt nature of having experienced something combines with the moral imperative to trust one's own experiences rather than be guided by tradition."[11]

Indeed, the experience tends to lead to moral decisions which are defended and trusted as valid and obviously require logical reasoning and interpretation. Pascal's declaration that religion has both outward and inward foundations repeats the recognition of the need for intellectual involvement in religious experience.[12] To define this profound necessity for cognitive understanding, Rudolf Otto, whose most famous work seeks to delineate and describe the ineffable numinous, writes that the experience of the Holy is

> irreducible to any other [state of mind]; and therefore, like every absolute primary and elementary datum, while it admits of being discussed, it cannot be strictly defined. There is only one way to help another to an understanding of it. He must be guided and led on by consideration and discussion of the matter through the ways of his own mind, until he reach the point at which [this profound awareness] in him perforce begins to stir, to start into life and into consciousness. We can cooperate in this process by bringing before his notice all that can be found in

---

11. Bregman, *Rediscovery*, 3.
12. Brown, *Psychology of Religion*, 115.

other regions of the mind, already known and familiar to resemble, or again to afford some special contrast to, the particular experience we wish to elucidate.¹³

Friedrich Schleiermacher, the strongest advocate in Western philosophical history for the importance of particular emotion in religion, realized that

> "he only who has studied and truly known man in these emotions can rediscover religion in all its outward manifestations."¹⁴

St. Thomas Aquinas asserted also that "it is fitting that [both the truth of reason and the truth of faith] be proposed to man divinely for belief."¹⁵ The inner experience of religious relationship with God cannot be scientifically measured but the pattern of experience exists in multiplicity since many millions of people in history claim to have religious conversions. Bouquet confirms the validity of the pattern-based analysis:

"Moreover, the intuitional experiences of the prophet, the seer, and the mystic need to be coordinated by comparison with the other types of evidence, and are accordingly guaranteed or invalidated by their discordance or harmony with the remainder of the date available. They must pass the test of coherence."¹⁶

Religious people, who may appear to be controlled or emotional, have their own perspectives on the priorities they give to their experience, belief, and faith, their own practice, and the formal sanctions of others. While individuals may be lost in, or set against, a religious system, they have seldom just "thought up" for themselves what it is they believe; it must be "found" or received.¹⁷

So, again, it appears necessary that a reasoned faith, one which considers personal and institutional perspectives, is the best approach to religion. The essence of religion is the experience;

13. Otto, *Idea of Holy*, 7.
14. Schleiermacher, *On Religion*, 16.
15. Miller, *Believing in God*, 31.
16. Bouquet, *Religious Experience*, 6.
17. Brown, *Psychology of Religion*, 17.

The Nature of Faith

one must share the experience to clearly understand or identify the nature of the incident. And we insist that understanding is a necessary part of a faith that remains vital. Cognitive rational explanations only go so far, but we expect them, at least to some degree, to give us security, assurance, and emotional stability. To use again the old example, those who have never fallen in love can talk about the phenomenon rationally but cannot "explain" or account for the emotion itself, the non-rational aspect of the experience and the sometimes strange behavior that accompanies it, until they experience the phenomenon for themselves. Bambi's lack of understanding and even rejection of the phenomenon in the Disney classic movie provides a good example. Once he, too, becomes "twitterpated," the confusion is removed. Afterwards, he can join others in the understanding, the rational discussion of the ineffable experience. Faith then, whether religious or scientific, must include the rational perspective about the truth of experience or the human interaction with reality becomes meaningless. But it is "faith" because we rely on some other source than our own senses to trust that the unseen reality exists.

8

What Does It Take to Build a World?

WITHOUT A VISION FOR the way a world should look, of course, no changes will be made to the one we have now. So first we must conceive of the "best of all possible worlds." The twenty-first century generation declares that a world can and must be built where conflicts cease. For that to happen, all cultures, groups, political philosophies, worldviews, and religions would have to agree to disagree amiably. The paradigms for discussions and applications of ideas would have to be changed from warfare models to journeys to truth, or at least to cooperation. A massive persuasion campaign, perhaps via media, would possibly generate enough mutual familiarity among cultures and groups to make everyone become assured that all groups are valuable and acceptable. The problem is that such a philosophy is relativism, which has never functioned ideally. The sinful inclinations and inherent selfishness of humans naturally aborts such an ideal possibility. Relativism always reduces to "might makes right" eventually. People want things, and when two or more people want the same thing, conflict emerges. The one with the power to get the desired object will assert himself and get it. Self-interest trumps altruism in most of the world.

In the twentieth century, some people believed that a one-world government could achieve the ideal. Such was the underlying notion of the European Union, socialist political theory, communism, utopianism, Far Eastern corporal psychology, and other futurist concepts (all of which have failed because of the inherent narcissistic selfish human perspective). Persuasion has failed to convince sufficient numbers of people, and government force eventually breeds revolution. People cannot be dealt with like cows nor do they like change enough to accept ideas totally foreign to their understanding of reality. Even understanding and appreciating other people and cultures does not mean that people will be glad to change themselves to accommodate counter-intuitive and non-traditional practices. The very ideas of diversity and multiculturalism create the struggle of living with each other in all countries.

The very essence of conflict with enemies, like recognizing the suffering in the world, provides us with the awareness that we need a rescuer, someone to "fix things." We are aware that the world should not be this way, that love is better than war, that poverty and hunger and disease don't belong in this world. But all our efforts over these several thousands of years wherein we have tried to make the world better have failed. Only one who is above and greater than we, and the world we live in, can solve the problems permanently. Our efforts, as good and justified as they are, merely patch a part of the wound.

We must also be aware that there are evil, cruel, and selfish people in the world who have no compassion or empathy for everyone else. Evil actions and intentions force us to oppose such things, creating conflict. Merely submitting to the evil eliminates our efforts toward peace and fairness. Gandhi and Martin Luther King Jr. succeeded because their efforts at non-violent civil disobedience appealed to the collective conscience of the populous of countries and laws with Christian foundations. We have seen, in the late twentieth and early twenty-first centuries, rulers and countries, founded on principles contrary to Christianity, that feel no regret of the killing of any people who disagree with them. This is not an era of revolution; this is the era of submission to the supposed moral responsibility of government to make decisions for its citizens. People just want peace and security rather than freedom. They have become addicts to affluence and leisure. Pain and fear are their worst enemies and they believe that cooperation, submission, and acceptance will dispel these anxieties. People who build a world have vision, courage, and leadership. We endeavor to imagine and envision the way a world should properly be. This post-modern world of the currently young seems to reflect their desire for security and peace,

> "Seeing is not believing . . . What we learn from experience depends on the kind of philosophy we bring to the experience. It is therefore useless to appeal to experience before we have settled, as well as we can, the philosophical question."[1]

Individuals who persist in living apart from biblical directives misinterpret their experience with God as approval of their lifestyles when, in fact, God wishes for them to repent and return to holy normality. Because we have experiences with God does not automatically sanction our worldviews, lifestyles, or ideas. Our experiences with God should make us seek him and his truth, which will cause us to abandon all views and practices which are not approved by him, as he has revealed the truth in Scripture. Misinterpreting Scripture occurs for the same reasons; we bring faulty philosophies to the task. Historical-critical biblical hermeneutic was not brought to scholarly circles by evil-intentioned persons, rather persons with faulty philosophies. People rationalize and justify all kinds of views with Scripture because their philosophies lead them; their hearts and minds are closed to the truth for the same reason. Good scholarship must begin with teachable minds of persons who want to know truth, whether that truth crushes their favorite philosophy or not. We are faulty beings; we need teaching all our lives. Our emotions must not lead us either. We may be led over the brink into opposition to God, even with sincere motivations, simply because our foundational philosophy overrides reality, the truth in God. Start with him and what he says

---

1. Lewis, *Miracles*, 1.

and what he wants. Learn what his nature is, what his character is, then approach the study of our pet notions with the distinct likelihood that we are wrong somewhere and let his nature determine the direction of our conclusions. We live in a world where every "wind of doctrine," and then some, floats over the visual and electronic waves in massive quantity, and we must assess these views to discover when truth appears. All the advocates of these views begin with a philosophical foundation of ideas and build from there. We must have the right philosophical foundation, built from Scripture and proper hermeneutical and logical methodology, and allow all messages to be sifted through that foundation first, before we decide where we should stand on any issue.

Christian life is like seeking butterflies. Pentecostals hop all around looking for the butterflies as they appear to flit from flower (church, meeting, or service) to flower. When they ask traditional Christians about butterflies, the traditional ones say, "Butterflies? Oh, you mean one of these?" as they pull one from their pockets. They have had butterflies all the time, but under other names.

The mind is a world. Reality depends on how we process it, as far as we are concerned. Our perceptions of the real, affected by our philosophical interpretations and mental constructions, clearly differ person to person. There is, I'm sure, an objective reality, but none of us can truly know its extent and breadth though we function in the reality that is available to us. God reveals certain aspects of reality to us, and even then, not all of us comprehend this revelation the same ways. In the mental world, things happen (experiences), the meanings of which we try to understand with the help of authorities, like books, articles, scholars, friends, family, and so on, but ultimately the way the mind computes and arranges all this data will determine our comprehension. Personality and training affect our processing system, thus allowing some bits of misinterpretation to slip in. It is amazing, really, that we mutually understand as much as we do. That is likely why people of similar upbringing, education, and social interaction seem to be comfortable together. They are most likely to understand the bits more like the other members of the group.

Enigmatic If Not Ineffable

Because the human mind is logical and reasonable, we can organize and structure entire systems of theories and ideas that "logically" flow from completely false presuppositions. We have been systematically brainwashed as a society to believe the absolute authority of empiricism and math as arbiters of all truth, simply because the results of such methodology "works" in the building of technology. That kind of pragmatic result is the demonstration of the limitations of the methodology—technology is what empiricism and math produce, but they are not the sources of ultimate truth.

Appendix
Evolution and Ethics
T.H. Huxley's Lecture 1893[1]

THERE IS A DELIGHTFUL child's story, known by the title of "Jack and the Bean-stalk," with which my contemporaries who are present will be familiar. But so many of our grave and reverend juniors have been brought up on severer intellectual diet, and, perhaps, have become acquainted with fairyland only through primers of comparative mythology, that it may be needful to give an outline of the tale. It is a legend of a bean-plant, which grows and grows until it reaches the high heavens and there spreads out into a vast canopy of foliage. The hero, being moved to climb the stalk, discovers that the leafy expanse supports a world composed of the same elements as that below, but yet strangely new; and his adventures there, on which I may not dwell, must have completely changed his views of the nature of things; though the story, not having been composed by, or for, philosophers, has nothing to say about views.

My present enterprise has a certain analogy to that of the daring adventurer. I beg you to accompany me in an attempt to reach a world which, to many, is probably strange, by the help of a bean. It is, as you know, a simple, inert looking thing. Yet, if planted under proper conditions, of which sufficient warmth is one of the most important, it manifests active powers of a very remarkable kind. A small green seedling emerges, rises to the surface of the

---

1. Huxley, "Evolution and Ethics,"

soil, rapidly increases in size and, at the same time, undergoes a series of metamorphoses which do not excite our wonder as much as those which meet us in legendary history, merely because they are to be seen every day and all day long.

By insensible steps, the plant builds itself up into a large and various fabric of root, stem, leaves, flowers, and fruit, every one molded within and without in accordance with an extremely complex but, at the same time, minutely defined pattern. In each of these complicated structures, as in their smallest constituents, there is an immanent energy which, in harmony with that resident in all the others, incessantly works towards the maintenance of the whole and the efficient performance of the part which it has to play in the economy of nature. But no sooner has the edifice, reared with such exact elaboration, attained completeness, than it begins to crumble. By degrees, the plant withers and disappears from view, leaving behind more or fewer apparently inert and simple bodies, just like the bean from which it sprang; and, like it, endowed with the potentiality of giving rise to a similar cycle of manifestations.

Neither the poetic nor the scientific imagination is put too much strain in the search after analogies with this process of going forth and, as it were, returning to the starting-point. It may be likened to the ascent and descent of a slung stone, or the course of an arrow along its trajectory. Or we may say that the living energy takes first an upward and then a downward road. Or it may seem preferable to compare the expansion of the germ into the full-grown plant, to the unfolding of a fan, or to the rolling forth and widening of a stream; and thus to arrive at the conception of "development," or "evolution." Here as elsewhere, names are "noise and smoke"; the important point is to have a clear and adequate conception of the fact signified by a name. And, in this case, the fact is the Sisyphæan process, in the course of which the living and growing plant passes from the relative simplicity and latent potentiality of the seed to the full epiphany of a highly differentiated type, thence to fall back to simplicity and potentiality.

Evolution and Ethics

The value of a strong intellectual grasp of the nature of this process lies in the circumstance that what is true of the bean is true of living things in general. From very low forms up to the highest—in the animal no less than in the vegetable kingdom—the process of life presents the same appearance of cyclical evolution. Nay, we have but to cast our eyes over the rest of the world and cyclical change presents itself on all sides. It meets us in the water that flows to the sea and returns to the springs; in the heavenly bodies that wax and wane, go and return to their places; in the inexorable sequence of the ages of man's life; in that successive rise, apogee, and fall of dynasties and of states which is the most prominent topic of civil history.

As no man fording a swift stream can dip his foot twice into the same water, so no man can, with exactness, affirm of anything in the sensible world that it is. As he utters the words, nay, as he thinks them, the predicate ceases to be applicable; the present has become the past; the "is" should be "was." And the more we learn of the nature of things, the more evident is it that what we call rest is only unperceived activity—that seeming peace is silent but strenuous battle. In every part, at every moment, the state of the cosmos is the expression of a transitory adjustment of contending forces, a scene of strife, in which all the combatants fall in turn. What is true of each part, is true of the whole. Natural knowledge tends more and more to the conclusion that "all the choir of heaven and furniture of the earth" are the transitory forms of parcels of cosmic substance wending along the road of evolution, from nebulous potentiality through endless growths of sun and planet and satellite; through all varieties of matter; through infinite diversities of life and thought; possibly, through modes of being of which we neither have a conception, nor are competent to form any, back to the indefinable latency from which they arose. Thus the most obvious attribute of the cosmos is its impermanence. It assumes the aspect not so much of a permanent entity as of a changeful process, in which naught endures save the flow of energy and the rational order which pervades it.

Appendix

We have climbed our bean-stalk and have reached a wonderland in which the common and the familiar become things new and strange. In the exploration of the cosmic process thus typified, the highest intelligence of man finds inexhaustible employment; giants are subdued to our service, and the spiritual affections of the contemplative philosopher are engaged by beauties worthy of eternal constancy.

But there is another aspect of the cosmic process, so perfect as a mechanism, so beautiful as a work of art. Where the cosmopoetic energy works through sentient beings, there arises, among its other manifestations, that which we call pain or suffering. This baleful product of evolution increases in quantity and in intensity, with advancing grades of animal organization, until it attains its highest level in man. Further, the consummation is not reached in man, the mere animal, nor in man, the whole or half savage, but only in man, the member of an organized polity. And it is a necessary consequence of his attempt to live in this way—that is, under those conditions which are essential to the full development of his noblest powers.

Man, the animal, in fact, has worked his way to the headship of the sentient world, and has become the superb animal which he is, in virtue of his success in the struggle for existence. The conditions having been of a certain order, man's organization has adjusted itself to them better than that of his competitors in the cosmic strife. In the case of mankind, the self-assertion, the unscrupulous seizing upon all that can be grasped, the tenacious holding of all that can be kept, which constitute the essence of the struggle for existence, have answered. For his successful progress, throughout the savage state, man has been largely indebted to those qualities which he shares with the ape and the tiger: his exceptional physical organization; his cunning, his sociability, his curiosity, and his imitativeness; his ruthless and ferocious destructiveness when his anger is roused by opposition.

But, in proportion as men have passed from anarchy to social organization, and in proportion as civilization has grown in worth, these deeply ingrained serviceable qualities have become defects.

After the manner of successful persons, civilized man would gladly kick down the ladder by which he has climbed. He would be only too pleased to see "the ape and tiger die." But they decline to suit his convenience; and the unwelcome intrusion of these boon companions of his hot youth into the ranged existence of civil life adds pains and griefs, innumerable and immeasurably great, to those which the cosmic process necessarily brings on the mere animal. In fact, civilized man brands all these ape and tiger promptings with the name of sins; he punishes many of the acts which flow from them as crimes; and, in extreme cases, he does his best to put an end to the survival of the fittest of former days by axe and rope.

I have said that civilized man has reached this point; the assertion is perhaps too broad and general; I had better put it that ethical man has attained thereto. The science of ethics professes to furnish us with a reasoned rule of life—to tell us what is right action and why it is so. Whatever differences of opinion may exist among experts, there is a general consensus that the ape and tiger methods of the struggle for existence are not reconcilable with sound ethical principles.

The hero of our story descended the bean-stalk and came back to the common world, where fare and work were alike hard, where ugly competitors were much commoner than beautiful princesses, and where the everlasting battle with self was much less sure to be crowned with victory than a turn-to with a giant. We have done the like. Thousands upon thousands of our fellows, thousands of years ago, have preceded us in finding themselves face to face with the same dread problem of evil. They also have seen that the cosmic process is evolution—that it is full of wonder, full of beauty, and, at the same time, full of pain. They have sought to discover the bearing of these great facts on ethics, to find out whether there is, or is not, a sanction for morality in the ways of the cosmos.

Theories of the universe, in which the conception of evolution plays a leading part, were extant at least six centuries before our era. Certain knowledge of them, in the fifth century, reaches us from localities as distant as the valley of the Ganges and the Asiatic

Appendix

coasts of the Ægean. To the early philosophers of Hindostan, no less than to those of Ionia, the salient and characteristic feature of the phenomenal world was its changefulness, the unresting flow of all things, through birth to visible being and thence to not being, in which they could discern no sign of a beginning and for which they saw no prospect of an ending. It was no less plain to some of these antique forerunners of modern philosophy that suffering is the badge of all the tribe of sentient things, that it is no accidental accompaniment, but an essential constituent of the cosmic process. The energetic Greek might find fierce joys in a world in which strife is father and king; but the old Aryan spirit was subdued to quietism in the Indian sage; the mist of suffering which spread over humanity hid everything else from his view; to him life was one with suffering and suffering with life.

In Hindostan, as in Ionia, a period of relatively high and tolerably stable civilization had succeeded long ages of semi-barbarism and struggle. Out of wealth and security had come leisure and refinement, and, close at their heels, had followed the malady of thought. To the struggle for bare existence, which never ends, though it may be alleviated and partially disguised for a fortunate few, succeeded the struggle to make existence intelligible and to bring the order of things into harmony with the moral sense of man, which also never ends, but, for the thinking few, becomes keener with every increase of knowledge and with every step towards the realization of a worthy ideal of life.

2,500 years ago, the value of civilization was as apparent as it is now; then, as now, it was obvious that only in the garden of an orderly polity can the finest fruits humanity is capable of bearing be produced. But it had also become evident that the blessings of culture were not unmixed. The garden was apt to turn into a hothouse. The stimulation of the senses and the pampering of the emotions endlessly multiplied the sources of pleasure. The constant widening of the intellectual field indefinitely extended the range of that, especially human faculty of looking before and after, which adds to the fleeting present of those old and new worlds of the past and the future, wherein men dwell more the higher their culture.

Evolution and Ethics

But that very sharpening of the sense and that subtle refinement of emotion, which brought such a wealth of pleasures, were fatally attended by a proportional enlargement of the capacity for suffering; and the divine faculty of imagination, while it created new heavens and new earths, provided them with the corresponding hells of futile regret for the past and morbid anxiety for the future. Finally, the inevitable penalty of over-stimulation and exhaustion opened the gates of civilization to its great enemy, ennui: the stale and flat weariness when man delights not, nor woman neither, when all things are vanity and vexation; and life seems not worth living except to escape the bore of dying.

Even purely intellectual progress brings about its revenges. Problems settled in a rough and ready way by rude men, absorbed in action, demand renewed attention and show themselves to be still unread riddles when men have time to think. The beneficent demon, doubt, whose name is Legion and who dwells amongst the tombs of old faiths, enters into mankind and thenceforth refuses to be cast out. Sacred customs, venerable dooms of ancestral wisdom, hallowed by tradition and professing to hold good for all time, are put to the question. Cultured reflection asks for their credentials; judges them by its own standards; finally, gathers those of which it approves into ethical systems, in which the reasoning is rarely much more than a decent pretext for the adoption of foregone conclusions.

One of the oldest and most important elements in such systems is the conception of justice. Society is impossible unless those who are associated agree to observe certain rules of conduct towards one another; its stability depends on the steadiness with which they abide by that agreement; and, so far as they waver, that mutual trust which is the bond of society is weakened or destroyed. Wolves could not hunt in packs except for the real, though unexpressed, understanding that they should not attack one another during the chase. The most rudimentary polity is a pack of men living under the like tacit, or expressed, understanding; and having made the very important advance upon wolf society, that they agree to use the force of the whole body against individuals who violate it and in favor of those who observe it. This observance of a common understanding, with the consequent distribution of punishments and rewards according to accepted rules, received the name of justice, while the contrary was called injustice. Early ethics did not take much note of the animus of the violator of the rules. But civilization could not advance far, without the establishment of a capital distinction between the case of involuntary and that of willful misdeed; between a merely wrong action and a guilty one. And, with increasing refinement of moral appreciation, the problem of desert, which arises out of this distinction, acquired more and more theoretical and practical importance. If life must be given for life, yet it was recognized that the unintentional slayer did not altogether deserve death; and, by a sort of compromise between the public and the private conception of justice, a sanctuary was provided in which he might take refuge from the avenger of blood.

The idea of justice thus underwent a gradual sublimation from punishment and reward according to acts, to punishment and reward according to desert; or, in other words, according to motive. Righteousness, that is, action from right motive, not only became synonymous with justice but the positive constituent of innocence and the very heart of goodness.

Now when the ancient sage, whether Indian or Greek, who had attained to this conception of goodness, looked the world, and especially human life, in the face, he found it as hard as we do to bring the course of evolution into harmony with even the elementary requirements of the ethical ideal of the just and the good.

If there is one thing plainer than another, it is that neither the pleasures nor the pains of life, in the merely animal world, are distributed according to desert; for it is admittedly impossible for the lower orders of sentient beings to deserve either the one or the other. If there is a generalization from the facts of human life which has the assent of thoughtful men in every age and country, it is that the violator of ethical rules constantly escapes the punishment which he deserves; that the wicked flourishes like a green bay tree, while the righteous begs his bread; that the sins of the

Evolution and Ethics

fathers are visited upon the children; that, in the realm of nature, ignorance is punished just as severely as willful wrong; and that thousands upon thousands of innocent beings suffer for the crime, or the unintentional trespass, of one.

Greek and Semite and Indian are agreed upon this subject. The book of Job is at one with the "Works and Days" and the Buddhist Sutras; the Psalmist and the Preacher of Israel, with the Tragic Poets of Greece. What is a more common motive of the ancient tragedy in fact, than the unfathomable injustice of the nature of things; what is more deeply felt to be true than its presentation of the destruction of the blameless by the work of his own hands, or by the fatal operation of the sins of others? Surely Œdipus was pure of heart; it was the natural sequence of events—the cosmic process—which drove him, in all innocence, to slay his father and become the husband of his mother, to the desolation of his people and his own headlong ruin. Or to step, for a moment, beyond the chronological limits I have set myself, what constitutes the sempiternal attraction of Hamlet but the appeal to deepest experience of that history of a no less blameless dreamer, dragged, in spite of himself, into a world out of joint; involved in a tangle of crime and misery, created by one of the prime agents of the cosmic process as it works in and through man?

Thus, brought before the tribunal of ethics, the cosmos might well seem to stand condemned. The conscience of man revolted against the moral indifference of nature, and the microcosmic atom should have found the illimitable macrocosm guilty. But few, or none, ventured to record that verdict.

In the great Semitic trial of this issue, Job takes refuge in silence and submission; the Indian and the Greek, less wise perhaps, attempt to reconcile the irreconcilable and plead for the defendant. To this end, the Greeks invented Theodicies; while the Indians devised what, in its ultimate form, must rather be termed a Cosmodicy. For, though Buddhism recognizes gods many and lords many, they are products of the cosmic process; and transitory, however long enduring, manifestations of its eternal activity. In the doctrine of transmigration, whatever its origin, Brahminical

Appendix

and Buddhist speculation found, ready to hand, the means of constructing a plausible vindication of the ways of the cosmos to man. If this world is full of pain and sorrow; if grief and evil fall, like the rain, upon both the just and the unjust; it is because, like the rain, they are links in the endless chain of natural causation by which past, present, and future are indissolubly connected; and there is no more injustice in the one case than in the other. Every sentient being is reaping as it has sown; if not in this life, then in one or other of the infinite series of antecedent existences of which it is the latest term. The present distribution of good and evil is, therefore, the algebraical sum of accumulated positive and negative deserts; or, rather, it depends on the floating balance of the account. For it was not thought necessary that a complete settlement should ever take place. Arrears might stand over as a sort of "hanging gale"; a period of celestial happiness just earned might be succeeded by ages of torment in a hideous nether world, the balance still overdue for some remote ancestral error.

Whether the cosmic process looks any more moral than at first, after such a vindication, may perhaps be questioned. Yet this plea of justification is not less plausible than others; and none but very hasty thinkers will reject it on the ground of inherent absurdity. Like the doctrine of evolution itself, that of transmigration has its roots in the world of reality; and it may claim such support as the great argument from analogy is capable of supplying.

Everyday experience familiarizes us with the facts which are grouped under the name of heredity. Every one of us bears upon him obvious marks of his parentage, perhaps of remoter relationships. More particularly, the sum of tendencies to act in a certain way, which we call "character," is often to be traced through a long series of progenitors and collaterals. So we may justly say that this "character"—this moral and intellectual essence of a man—does veritably pass over from one fleshly tabernacle to another, and does really transmigrate from generation to generation. In the newborn infant, the character of the stock lies latent, and the Ego is little more than a bundle of potentialities. But, very early, these become actualities; from childhood to age they manifest themselves

Evolution and Ethics

in dullness or brightness, weakness or strength, viciousness or uprightness; and with each feature modified by confluence with another character, if by nothing else, the character passes on to its incarnation in new bodies.

The Indian philosophers called character, as thus defined, "karma." It is this karma which passed from life to life and linked them in the chain of transmigrations; and they held that it is modified in each life, not merely by confluence of parentage, but by its own acts. They were, in fact, strong believers in the theory, so much disputed just at present, of the hereditary transmission of acquired characters. That the manifestation of the tendencies of a character may be greatly facilitated, or impeded, by conditions, of which self-discipline, or the absence of it, are among the most important, is indubitable; but that the character itself is modified in this way is by no means so certain; it is not so sure that the transmitted character of an evil liver is worse, or that of a righteous man better, than that which he received. Indian philosophy, however, did not admit of any doubt on this subject; the belief in the influence of conditions, notably of self-discipline, on the karma was not merely a necessary postulate of its theory of retribution, but it presented the only way of escape from the endless round of transmigrations.

The earlier forms of Indian philosophy agreed with those prevalent in our own times, in supposing the existence of a permanent reality, or "substance," beneath the shifting series of phenomena, whether of matter or of mind. The substance of the cosmos was "Brahma," that of the individual man "Atman"; and the latter was separated from the former only, if I may so speak, by its phenomenal envelope, by the casing of sensations, thoughts and desires, pleasures and pains, which make up the illusive phantasmagoria of life. This the ignorant take for reality; their "Atman" therefore remains eternally imprisoned in delusions, bound by the fetters of desire and scourged by the whip of misery. But the man who has attained enlightenment sees that the apparent reality is mere illusion, or, as was said a couple of thousand years later, that there is nothing good nor bad but thinking makes it so. If the cosmos "is just and of our pleasant vices makes instruments to scourge us," it

Appendix

would seem that the only way to escape from our heritage of evil is to destroy that fountain of desire whence our vices flow; to refuse any longer to be the instruments of the evolutionary process, and withdraw from the struggle for existence. If the karma is modifiable by self-discipline, if its coarser desires, one after another, can be extinguished, the ultimate fundamental desire of self-assertion, or the desire to be, may also be destroyed. Then the bubble of illusion will burst, and the freed individual "Atman" will lose itself in the universal "Brahma."

Such seems to have been the pre-Buddhistic conception of salvation, and of the way to be followed by those who would attain thereto. No more thorough mortification of the flesh has ever been attempted than that achieved by the Indian ascetic anchorite; no later monachism has so nearly succeeded in reducing the human mind to that condition of impassive quasi-somnambulism, which, but for its acknowledged holiness, might run the risk of being confounded with idiocy.

And this salvation, it will be observed, was to be attained through knowledge, and by action based on that knowledge; just as the experimenter, who would obtain a certain physical or chemical result, must have a knowledge of the natural laws involved and the persistent disciplined will adequate to carry out all the various operations required. The supernatural, in our sense of the term, was entirely excluded. There was no external power which could affect the sequence of cause and effect which gives rise to karma; none but the will of the subject of the karma which could put an end to it.

Only one rule of conduct could be based upon the remarkable theory of which I have endeavored to give a reasoned outline. It was folly to continue to exist when an overplus of pain was certain; and the probabilities in favor of the increase of misery with the prolongation of existence, were so overwhelming. Slaying the body only made matters worse; there was nothing for it but to slay the soul by the voluntary arrest of all its activities. Property, social ties, family affections, common companionship, must be abandoned; the most natural appetites, even that for food, must be suppressed, or at least minimized; until all that remained of a man was the impassive, extenuated, mendicant monk, self-hypnotized into cataleptic trances, which the deluded mystic took for foretastes of the final union with Brahma.

The founder of Buddhism accepted the chief postulates demanded by his predecessors. But he was not satisfied with the practical annihilation involved in merging the individual existence in the unconditioned—the Atman in Brahma. It would seem that the admission of the existence of any substance whatever—even of the tenuity of that which has neither quality nor energy and of which no predicate whatever can be asserted—appeared to him to be a danger and a snare. Though reduced to a hypostatized negation, Brahma was not to be trusted; so long as entity was there, it might conceivably resume the weary round of evolution, with all its train of immeasurable miseries. Gautama got rid of even that shade of a shadow of permanent existence by a metaphysical *tour de force* of great interest to the student of philosophy, seeing that it supplies the wanting half of Bishop Berkeley's well-known idealistic argument.

Granting the premises, I am not aware of any escape from Berkeley's conclusion, that the "substance" of matter is a metaphysical unknown quantity, of the existence of which there is no proof. What Berkeley does not seem to have so clearly perceived is that the non-existence of a substance of mind is equally arguable; and that the result of the impartial applications of his reasonings is the reduction of the All to co-existences and sequences of phenomena, beneath and beyond which there is nothing cognoscible. It is a remarkable indication of the subtlety of Indian speculation that Gautama should have seen deeper than the greatest of modern idealists; though it must be admitted that, if some of Berkeley's reasonings respecting the nature of spirit are pushed home, they reach pretty much the same conclusion.

Accepting the prevalent Brahminical doctrine that the whole cosmos, celestial, terrestrial, and infernal, with its population of gods and other celestial beings, of sentient animals, of Mara and his devils, is incessantly shifting through recurring cycles of production and destruction, in each of which every human being has his transmigratory representative, Gautama proceeded to eliminate substance altogether; and to reduce the cosmos to a mere flow of sensations, emotions, volitions, and thoughts, devoid of any substratum. As, on the surface of a stream of water, we see ripples and whirlpools, which last for a while and then vanish with the causes that gave rise to them, so what seem individual existences are mere temporary associations of phenomena circling round a center, "like a dog tied to a post." In the whole universe there is nothing permanent, no eternal substance either of mind or of matter. Personality is a metaphysical fancy; and in very truth, not only we, but all things, in the worlds without end of the cosmic phantasmagoria, are such stuff as dreams are made of.

What then becomes of karma? Karma remains untouched. As the peculiar form of energy we call magnetism may be transmitted from a loadstone to a piece of steel, from the steel to a piece of nickel, as it may be strengthened or weakened by the conditions to which it is subjected while resident in each piece, so it seems to have been conceived that karma might be transmitted from one phenomenal association to another by a sort of induction. However this may be, Gautama doubtless had a better guarantee for the abolition of transmigration, when no wrack of substance, either of Atman or of Brahma, was left behind when, in short, a man had but to dream that he willed not to dream, to put an end to all dreaming.

This end of life's dream is Nirvana. What Nirvana is the learned do not agree. But, since the best original authorities tell us there is neither desire nor activity, nor any possibility of phenomenal reappearance for the sage who has entered Nirvana, it may be safely said of this acme of Buddhistic philosophy—"the rest is silence."

Thus there is no very great practical disagreement between Gautama and his predecessors with respect to the end of action; but it is otherwise as regards the means to that end. With just insight into human nature, Gautama declared extreme ascetic practices to be useless and indeed harmful. The appetites and the passions

Evolution and Ethics

are not to be abolished by mere mortification of the body; they must, in addition, be attacked on their own ground and conquered by steady cultivation of the mental habits which oppose them; by universal benevolence; by the return of good for evil; by humility; by abstinence from evil thought; in short, by total renunciation of that self-assertion which is the essence of the cosmic process.

Doubtless, it is to these ethical qualities that Buddhism owes its marvelous success. A system which knows no God in the western sense; which denies a soul to man; which counts the belief in immortality a blunder and the hope of it a sin; which refuses any efficacy to prayer and sacrifice; which bids men look to nothing but their own efforts for salvation; which, in its original purity, knew nothing of vows of obedience, abhorred intolerance, and never sought the aid of the secular arm; yet spread over a considerable moiety of the Old World with marvelous rapidity, and is still, with whatever base admixture of foreign superstitions, the dominant creed of a large fraction of mankind.

Let us now set our faces westwards, towards Asia Minor and Greece and Italy, to view the rise and progress of another philosophy, apparently independent, but no less pervaded by the conception of evolution.

The sages of Miletus were pronounced evolutionists; and, however dark may be some of the sayings of Heraclitus of Ephesus, who was probably a contemporary of Gautama, no better expressions of the essence of the modern doctrine of evolution can be found than are presented by some of his pithy aphorisms and striking metaphors. Indeed, many of my present auditors must have observed that, more than once, I have borrowed from him in the brief exposition of the theory of evolution with which this discourse commenced.

But when the focus of Greek intellectual activity shifted to Athens, the leading minds concentrated their attention upon ethical problems. Forsaking the study of the macrocosm for that of the microcosm, they lost the key to the thought of the great Ephesian, which, I imagine, is more intelligible to us than it was to Socrates, or to Plato. Socrates, more especially, set the fashion of a kind of inverse agnosticism, by teaching that the problems of physics lie beyond the reach of the human intellect; that the attempt to solve them is essentially vain; that the one worthy object of investigation is the problem of ethical life; and his example was followed by the Cynics and the later Stoics. Even the comprehensive knowledge and the penetrating intellect of Aristotle failed to suggest to him that in holding the eternity of the world, within its present range of mutation, he was making a retrogressive step. The scientific heritage of Heraclitus passed into the hands neither of Plato nor of Aristotle, but into those of Democritus. But the world was not yet ready to receive the great conceptions of the philosopher of Abdera. It was reserved for the Stoics to return to the track marked out by the earlier philosophers; and, professing themselves disciples of Heraclitus, to develop the idea of evolution systematically. In doing this, they not only omitted some characteristic features of their master's teaching, but they made additions altogether foreign to it. One of the most influential of these importations was the transcendental theism which had come into vogue. The restless, fiery energy, operating according to law, out of which all things emerge and into which they return, in the endless successive cycles of the great year; which creates and destroys worlds as a wanton child builds up, and anon levels, sand castles on the seashore; was metamorphosed into a material world-soul and decked out with all the attributes of ideal Divinity; not merely with infinite power and transcendent wisdom, but with absolute goodness.

The consequences of this step were momentous. For if the cosmos is the effect of an immanent, omnipotent, and infinitely beneficent cause, the existence in it of real evil, still less of necessarily inherent evil, is plainly inadmissible. Yet the universal experience of mankind testified then, as now, that, whether we look within us or without us, evil stares us in the face on all sides; that if anything is real, pain and sorrow and wrong are realities.

It would be a new thing in history if *a priori* philosophers were daunted by the factious opposition of experience; and the Stoics were the last men to allow themselves to be beaten by mere facts. "Give me a doctrine and I will find the reasons for it," said

Chrysippus. So they perfected, if they did not invent, that ingenious and plausible form of pleading, the Theodicy; for the purpose of showing firstly, that there is no such thing as evil; secondly, that if there is, it is the necessary correlate of good; and, moreover, that it is either due to our own fault, or inflicted for our benefit. Theodicies have been very popular in their time, and I believe that a numerous, though somewhat dwarfed, progeny of them still survives. So far as I know, they are all variations of the theme set forth in those famous six lines of the "Essay on Man," in which Pope sums up Bolingbroke's reminiscences of stoical and other speculations of this kind—

> "All nature is but art, unknown to thee;
> All chance, direction which thou canst not see;
> All discord, harmony not understood;
> All partial evil, universal good;
> And spite of pride, in erring reason's spite
> One truth is clear: whatever is, is right."

Yet, surely, if there are few more important truths than those enunciated in the first triad, the second is open to very grave objections. That there is a "soul of good in things evil" is unquestionable; nor will any wise man deny the disciplinary value of pain and sorrow. But these considerations do not help us to see why the immense multitude of irresponsible sentient beings, which cannot profit by such discipline, should suffer; nor why, among the endless possibilities open to omnipotence—that of sinless, happy existence among the rest—the actuality in which sin and misery abound should be that selected. Surely it is mere cheap rhetoric to call arguments which have never yet been answered by even the meekest and the least rational of Optimists, suggestions of the pride of reason. As to the concluding aphorism, its fittest place would be as an inscription in letters of mud over the portal of some "stye of Epicurus"; for that is where the logical application of it to practice would land men, with every aspiration stifled and every effort paralyzed. Why try to set right what is right already? Why strive to improve the best of all possible worlds? Let us eat and drink, for as today all is right, so to-morrow all will be.

But the attempt of the Stoics to blind themselves to the reality of evil, as a necessary concomitant of the cosmic process, had less success than that of the Indian philosophers to exclude the reality of good from their purview. Unfortunately, it is much easier to shut one's eyes to good than to evil. Pain and sorrow knock at our doors more loudly than pleasure and happiness; and the prints of their heavy footsteps are less easily effaced. Before the grim realities of practical life the pleasant fictions of optimism vanished. If this were the best of all possible worlds, it nevertheless proved itself a very inconvenient habitation for the ideal sage.

The stoical summary of the whole duty of man, "Live according to nature," would seem to imply that the cosmic process is an exemplar for human conduct. Ethics would thus become applied Natural History. In fact, a confused employment of the maxim, in this sense, has done immeasurable mischief in later times. It has furnished an axiomatic foundation for the philosophy of philosophasters and for the moralizing of sentimentalists. But the Stoics were, at bottom, not merely noble, but sane, men; and if we look closely into what they really meant by this ill-used phrase, it will be found to present no justification for the mischievous conclusions that have been deduced from it.

In the language of the Stoa, "Nature" was a word of many meanings. There was the "Nature" of the cosmos and the "Nature" of man. In the latter, the animal "nature," which man shares with a moiety of the living part of the cosmos, was distinguished from a higher "nature." Even in this higher nature there were grades of rank. The logical faculty is an instrument which may be turned to account for any purpose. The passions and the emotions are so closely tied to the lower nature that they may be considered to be pathological, rather than normal, phenomena. The one supreme, hegemonic, faculty, which constitutes the essential "nature" of man, is most nearly represented by that which, in the language of a later philosophy, has been called the pure reason. It is this "nature" which holds up the ideal of the supreme good

Evolution and Ethics

and demands absolute submission of the will to its behests. It is this which commands all men to love one another, to return good for evil, to regard one another as fellow-citizens of one great state. Indeed, seeing that the progress towards perfection of a civilized state, or polity, depends on the obedience of its members to these commands, the Stoics sometimes termed the pure reason the "political" nature. Unfortunately, the sense of the adjective has undergone so much modification, that the application of it to that which commands the sacrifice of self to the common good would now sound almost grotesque.

But what part is played by the theory of evolution in this view of ethics? So far as I can discern, the ethical system of the Stoics, which is essentially intuitive, and reverences the categorical imperative as strongly as that of any later moralists, might have been just what it was if they had held any other theory; whether that of special creation, on the one side, or that of the eternal existence of the present order, on the other. To the Stoic, the cosmos had no importance for the conscience, except in so far as he chose to think it a pedagogue to virtue. The pertinacious optimism of our philosophers hid from them the actual state of the case. It prevented them from seeing that cosmic nature is no school of virtue, but the headquarters of the enemy of ethical nature. The logic of facts was necessary to convince them that the cosmos works through the lower nature of man, not for righteousness, but against it. And it finally drove them to confess that the existence of their ideal "wise man" was incompatible with the nature of things; that even a passable approximation to that ideal was to be attained only at the cost of renunciation of the world and mortification, not merely of the flesh, but of all human affections. The state of perfection was that "apatheia" in which desire, though it may still be felt, is powerless to move the will, reduced to the sole function of executing the commands of pure reason. Even this residuum of activity was to be regarded as a temporary loan, as an efflux of the divine world-pervading spirit, chafing at its imprisonment in the flesh, until such time as death enabled it to return to its source in the all-pervading logos.

Appendix

I find it difficult to discover any very great difference between Apatheia and Nirvana, except that stoical speculation agrees with pre-Buddhistic philosophy, rather than with the teachings of Gautama, in so far as it postulates a permanent substance equivalent to "Brahma" and "Atman"; and that, in stoical practice, the adoption of the life of the mendicant cynic was held to be more a counsel of perfection than an indispensable condition of the higher life.

Thus the extremes touch. Greek thought and Indian thought set out from ground common to both, diverge widely, develop under very different physical and moral conditions, and finally converge to practically the same end.

The Vedas and the Homeric epos set before us a world of rich and vigorous life, full of joyous fighting men

> "That ever with a frolic welcome took
> The thunder and the sunshine . . ."

and who were ready to brave the very Gods themselves when their blood was up. A few centuries pass away, and under the influence of civilization the descendants of these men are "sicklied o'er with the pale cast of thought"—frank pessimists, or, at best, make-believe optimists. The courage of the warlike stock may be as hardly tried as before, perhaps more hardly, but the enemy is self. The hero has become a monk. The man of action is replaced by the quietist, whose highest aspiration is to be the passive instrument of the divine Reason. By the Tiber, as by the Ganges, ethical man admits that the cosmos is too strong for him; and, destroying every bond which ties him to it by ascetic discipline, he seeks salvation in absolute renunciation.

Modern thought is making a fresh start from the base whence Indian and Greek philosophy set out; and, the human mind being very much what it was six-and-twenty centuries ago, there is no ground for wonder if it presents indications of a tendency to move along the old lines to the same results.

We are more than sufficiently familiar with modern pessimism, at least as a speculation; for I cannot call to mind that any of its present votaries have sealed their faith by assuming the rags and the bowl of the mendicant Bhikku, or the cloak and the wallet of the Cynic. The obstacles placed in the way of sturdy vagrancy by an unphilosophical police have, perhaps, proved too formidable for philosophical consistency. We also know modern speculative optimism, with its perfectibility of the species, reign of peace, and lion and lamb transformation scenes; but one does not hear so much of it as one did forty years ago; indeed, I imagine it is to be met with more commonly at the tables of the healthy and wealthy, than in the congregations of the wise. The majority of us, I apprehend, profess neither pessimism nor optimism. We hold that the world is neither so good, nor so bad, as it conceivably might be; and, as most of us have reason, now and again, to discover that it can be. Those who have failed to experience the joys that make life worth living are, probably, in as small a minority as those who have never known the griefs that rob existence of its savor and turn its richest fruits into mere dust and ashes.

Further, I think I do not err in assuming that, however diverse their views on philosophical and religious matters, most men are agreed that the proportion of good and evil in life may be very sensibly affected by human action. I never heard anybody doubt that the evil may be thus increased, or diminished; and it would seem to follow that good must be similarly susceptible of addition or subtraction. Finally, to my knowledge, nobody professes to doubt that, so far forth as we possess a power of bettering things, it is our paramount duty to use it and to train all our intellect and energy to this supreme service of our kind.

Hence the pressing interest of the question, to what extent modern progress in natural knowledge, and, more especially, the general outcome of that progress in the doctrine of evolution, is competent to help us in the great work of helping one another?

The propounders of what are called the "ethics of evolution," when the "evolution of ethics" would usually better express the object of their speculations, adduce a number of more or less interesting facts and more or less sound arguments in favor of the origin of the moral sentiments, in the same way as other natural phenomena, by a process of evolution. I have little doubt, for my

Appendix

own part, that they are on the right track; but as the immoral sentiments have no less been evolved, there is, so far, as much natural sanction for the one as the other. The thief and the murderer follow nature just as much as the philanthropist. Cosmic evolution may teach us how the good and the evil tendencies of man may have come about; but, in itself, it is incompetent to furnish any better reason why what we call good is preferable to what we call evil than we had before. Someday, I doubt not, we shall arrive at an understanding of the evolution of the æsthetic faculty; but all the understanding in the world will neither increase nor diminish the force of the intuition that this is beautiful and that is ugly.

There is another fallacy which appears to me to pervade the so-called "ethics of evolution." It is the notion that because, on the whole, animals and plants have advanced in perfection of organization by means of the struggle for existence and the consequent "survival of the fittest"; therefore men in society, men as ethical beings, must look to the same process to help them towards perfection. I suspect that this fallacy has arisen out of the unfortunate ambiguity of the phrase "survival of the fittest." "Fittest" has a connotation of "best"; and about "best" there hangs a moral flavor. In cosmic nature, however, what is "fittest"f depends upon the conditions. Long since, I ventured to point out that if our hemisphere were to cool again, the survival of the fittest might bring about, in the vegetable kingdom, a population of more and more stunted and humbler and humbler organisms, until the "fittest" that survived might be nothing but lichens, diatoms, and such microscopic organisms as those which give red snow its color; while, if it became hotter, the pleasant valleys of the Thames and Isis might be uninhabitable by any animated beings save those that flourish in a tropical jungle. They, as the fittest, the best adapted to the changed conditions, would survive.

Men in society are undoubtedly subject to the cosmic process. As among other animals, multiplication goes on without cessation, and involves severe competition for the means of support. The struggle for existence tends to eliminate those less fitted to adapt themselves to the circumstances of their existence. The strongest, the most self-assertive, tend to tread down the weaker. But the influence of the cosmic process on the evolution of society is the greater the more rudimentary its civilization. Social progress means a checking of the cosmic process at every step and the substitution for it of another, which may be called the ethical process; the end of which is not the survival of those who may happen to be the fittest, in respect of the whole of the conditions which obtain, but of those who are ethically the best.

As I have already urged, the practice of that which is ethically best—what we call goodness or virtue—involves a course of conduct which, in all respects, is opposed to that which leads to success in the cosmic struggle for existence. In place of ruthless self-assertion it demands self-restraint; in place of thrusting aside, or treading down, all competitors, it requires that the individual shall not merely respect, but shall help his fellows; its influence is directed, not so much to the survival of the fittest, as to the fitting of as many as possible to survive. It repudiates the gladiatorial theory of existence. It demands that each man who enters into the enjoyment of the advantages of a polity shall be mindful of his debt to those who have laboriously constructed it; and shall take heed that no act of his weakens the fabric in which he has been permitted to live. Laws and moral precepts are directed to the end of curbing the cosmic process and reminding the individual of his duty to the community, to the protection and influence of which he owes, if not existence itself, at least the life of something better than a brutal savage.

It is from neglect of these plain considerations that the fanatical individualism of our time attempts to apply the analogy of cosmic nature to society. Once more we have a misapplication of the stoical injunction to follow nature; the duties of the individual to the state are forgotten, and his tendencies to self-assertion are dignified by the name of rights. It is seriously debated whether the members of a community are justified in using their combined strength to constrain one of their number to contribute his share to the maintenance of it; or even to prevent him from doing his best to destroy it. The struggle for existence, which has done such

Appendix

admirable work in cosmic nature, must, it appears, be equally beneficent in the ethical sphere. Yet if that which I have insisted upon is true; if the cosmic process has no sort of relation to moral ends; if the imitation of it by man is inconsistent with the first principles of ethics; what becomes of this surprising theory?

Let us understand, once for all, that the ethical progress of society depends, not on imitating the cosmic process, still less in running away from it, but in combating it. It may seem an audacious proposal thus to pit the microcosm against the macrocosm and to set man to subdue nature to his higher ends; but I venture to think that the great intellectual difference between the ancient times with which we have been occupied and our day, lies in the solid foundation we have acquired for the hope that such an enterprise may meet with a certain measure of success.

The history of civilization details the steps by which men have succeeded in building up an artificial world within the cosmos. Fragile reed as he may be, man, as Pascal says, is a thinking reed. There lies within him a fund of energy, operating intelligently and so far akin to that which pervades the universe, that it is competent to influence and modify the cosmic process. In virtue of his intelligence, the dwarf bends the Titan to his will. In every family, in every polity that has been established, the cosmic process in man has been restrained and otherwise modified by law and custom; in surrounding nature, it has been similarly influenced by the art of the shepherd, the agriculturist, the artisan. As civilization has advanced, so has the extent of this interference increased; until the organized and highly developed sciences and arts of the present day have endowed man with a command over the course of non-human nature greater than that once attributed to the magicians. The most impressive, I might say startling, of these changes have been brought about in the course of the last two centuries; while a right comprehension of the process of life and of the means of influencing its manifestations is only just dawning upon us. We do not yet see our way beyond generalities and we are befogged by the obtrusion of false analogies and crude anticipations. But Astronomy, Physics, Chemistry, have all had to pass through similar phases, before they reached the stage at which their influence became an important factor in human affairs. Physiology, Psychology, Ethics, Political Science, must submit to the same ordeal. Yet it seems to me irrational to doubt that, at no distant period, they will work as great a revolution in the sphere of practice.

The theory of evolution encourages no millennial anticipations. If, for millions of years, our globe has taken the upward road, yet, some time, the summit will be reached and the downward route will be commenced. The most daring imagination will hardly venture upon the suggestion that the power and the intelligence of man can ever arrest the procession of the great year.

Moreover, the cosmic nature born with us and, to a large extent, necessary for our maintenance, is the outcome of millions of years of severe training, and it would be folly to imagine that a few centuries will suffice to subdue its masterfulness to purely ethical ends. Ethical nature may count upon having to reckon with a tenacious and powerful enemy as long as the world lasts. But, on the other hand, I see no limit to the extent to which intelligence and will, guided by sound principles of investigation, and organized in common effort, may modify the conditions of existence, for a period longer than that now covered by history. And much may be done to change the nature of man himself. The intelligence which has converted the brother of the wolf into the faithful guardian of the flock ought to be able to do something towards curbing the instincts of savagery in civilized men.

But if we may permit ourselves a larger hope of abatement of the essential evil of the world than was possible to those who, in the infancy of exact knowledge, faced the problem of existence more than a score of centuries ago, I deem it an essential condition of the realization of that hope that we should cast aside the notion that the escape from pain and sorrow is the proper object of life.

We have long since emerged from the heroic childhood of our race, when good and evil could be met with the same "frolic welcome"; the attempts to escape from evil, whether Indian or Greek, have ended in flight from the battle-field; it remains to us to throw aside the youthful overconfidence and the no less youthful

Appendix

discouragement of nonage. We are grown men, and must play the man

> "strong in will
> To strive, to seek, to find, and not to yield,"

cherishing the good that falls in our way, and bearing the evil, in and around us, with stout hearts set on diminishing it. So far, we all may strive in one faith towards one hope:

> "It may be that the gulfs will wash us down,
> It may be we shall touch the Happy Isles,
> ... but something ere the end,
> Some work of noble note may yet be done."

Bibliography

Amery, Colin. "Meeting with John Ralston." *Philosophy Pathways 44* (November 3, 2002) (online only), https://philosophypathways.com/newsletter/issue44.html.
Armstrong, A.H. *An Introduction to Ancient Philosophy*. Boston: Beacon, 1959.
Barham, James. "Why I Am Not a Darwinist." In *Uncommon Dissent*, edited by William A. Dembski, 177–94. Wilmington, DE: ISI, 2004.
Beauchamp, Tom L. *Philosophical Ethics: An Introduction to Moral Philosophy*. Boston: McGraw-Hill, 2001.
Behe, Michael. "A Catholic Scientist Looks at Darwinism." In *Uncommon Dissent*, edited by William A. Dembski, 133–52. Wilmington, DE: ISI, 2004.
Bergamini, David. *Mathematics*. The Time Life Science Library. New York: Time Incorporated, 1963.
Berlinski, David. "The Deniable Darwin." In *Uncommon Dissent*, edited by William A. Dembski, 263–306. Wilmington, DE: ISI, 2004.
———. "God, Man, and Physics." *David Berlinski* (blog), the weekly Standard, February 18, 2002, https://www.weeklystandard.com/david-berlinski/god-man-and-physics.
Bouquet, A.C. *Religious Experience: Its Nature, Types, and Validity*. Westport, CT: Greenwood, 1968.
Bregman, Lucy. *The Rediscovery of the Inner Experience*. Chicago: Nelson Hall, 1982.
Bronowski, J. *The Ascent of Man*. London: BBC, 1975.
Brown, L.B. *The Psychology of Religion*. London: SPCK, 1988.
Budziszewski, J. "Accept No Limitations: The Rivalry of Naturalism and Natural Law." In *Uncommon Dissent*, edited by William A. Dembski, 99–114. Wilmington, DE: ISI, 2004.
Card, Orson Scott. *Children of the Mind*. New York: Tom Doherty Associates, 1996.
———. *Xenocide*. New York: Tom Doherty Associates, 1992.
Chapman, Geoff. *Guide to Transitional Fossils*. London: Creation Resources Trust, 2006.
Craig, William Lane and Richard Taylor. "Is the Basis of Morality Natural or Supernatural?" www.leaderu.com/offices/billcraig/docs/craig-tayloro.html.
Darwin, Charles. *The Origin of Species*. Oxford: Oxford University Press, 1998.

Bibliography

Dawkins, Richard. *A Devil's Chaplain*. London: Phoenix, 2004.
Delahunt, Michael. "Imagination." In the *ArtLex Visual Arts Dictionary*, 2002. www.proz.com/translation-glossary-post/English/4362.
Dembski, William A., ed. *Uncommon Dissent: Intellectuals Who Find Darwinism Unconvincing*. Wilmington, DE: ISI, 2004.
Fox, James. "Anthropomorphism, Anthropomorphites." *Catholic Encyclopedia* (blog), *New Advent*, http://www.newadvent.org/cathen/01558c.htm.
Freeman, Kathleen. *Ancilla to the Pre-Socratic Philosophers: A Complete Translation of the Fragments in Diels, Fragmente der Vorsokratiker*. Cambridge, MA: Harvard University Press, 1962.
———. *The Pre-Socratic Philosophers: A Companion to Diels, Fragmente der Vorsokratiker*. Cambridge, MA: Harvard University Press, 1959.
Geisler, Norman. *Baker's Encyclopedia of Christian Apologetics*. Grand Rapids: Baker, 1999.
Gorman, Christine. "The Brain: Six Lessons for Handling Stress." *Time*, January 19, 2007, http://content.time.com/time/magazine/article/0,9171, 1580401,00.html.
Gould, Stephen Jay. *Eight Little Piggies: Reflections in Natural History*. London: Penguin, 1993.
Grave, S.A. *The Scottish Philosophy of Common Sense*. Oxford: Clarendon, 1960.
Gribbin, John. *The Omega Point: The Search for the Missing Mass and the Ultimate Fate of the Universe*. London: Heinemann, 1987.
Gullberg, Jan. *Mathematics from the Birth of Numbers*. New York: Norton, 1997.
Guthrie, W.K.C. *A History of Greek Philosophy: Volume I*. Cambridge: The University Press, 1962.
Haig, Scott. "The Brain: The Power of Hope." *Time*, January 29, 2007, http://content.time.com/time/magazine/article/0,9171,1580392,00.html.
Hastings, James, ed. *Encyclopedia of Religion and Ethics*. Edinburgh: T. & T. Clark, 1912.
Hempel, Carl G. *Philosophy of Natural Science*. Englewood Cliffs, NJ: Prentice-Hall, 1966.
Hirsch, Roland F. "Darwinian Evolutionary Theory and the Life Sciences in the Twenty-First Century." In *Uncommon Dissent*, edited by William A. Dembski, 215–32. Wilmington, DE: ISI, 2004.
Howard, Roland. *Shopping for God: A Sceptic's Search for Value in the Spiritual Marketplace*. London: HarperCollins, 2001.
Hunter, Cornelius G. "Why Evolution Fails the Test of Science." In *Uncommon Dissent*, edited by William A. Dembski, 195–214. Wilmington, DE: ISI, 2004.
Hutton, Sarah. "The Cambridge Platonists." *Entries* (blog), *Stanford Encyclopedia of Philosophy*, October 3, 2001, https://plato.stanford.edu/entries/cambridge-platonists/.
Huxley, Julian. *Religion Without Revelation*. London: Watts and Company, 1945.

Bibliography

Huxley, Thomas Henry. "Evolution and Ethics." In *Readings in Philosophy*, edited by John Herman Randall, Justus Buchler, and Evelyn U. Shirk, 221–38. New York. Barnes and Noble, 1967.
Isaacs, Alan. *The Survival of God in the Scientific Age*. Middlesex, England: Penguin, 1966.
Jacquette, Dale. *Philosophy of Mind*. Prentice-Hall Foundations of Philosophy Series. Englewood Cliffs, NJ: Prentice-Hall, 1994.
James, William. *The Varieties of Religious Experience*. New York: Collier, 1961.
Johnson, Paul F. "Antipodes: Plato, Nietzsche, and the Moral Dimension of Leadership." http://ela.nmsu.edu/files/2013/07/antipodescondensed.pdf.
Jones, Steve. *Almost Like a Whale: The Origin of Species Updated*. London: Anchor, 2000.
Kant, Immanuel. *Foundations of the Metaphysics of Morals*. Indianapolis: Bobbs-Merrill, 1959.
Kim, Shin. "Moral Realism." M (blog), *Internet Encyclopedia of Philosophy*, https://www.iep.utm/.edu/moralrea/.
Kluger, Jeffrey. "The New Map of the Brain." *Time*, January 18, 2007, http://content.time.com/time/magazine/article/0,9171,1580416,00.html.
Kroner, Richard. *Speculation in Pre-Christian Philosophy*. London: Longmans, Green, and Co., 1957.
Kuhn, Thomas. *The Structure of Scientific Revolutions*. New York: New American Library and University of Chicago Press, 1986.
Landauer, Jeff and Joseph Rowlands. "Subjective Value." *Evil Ethics* (blog), *Importance of Philosophy*, 2001, www.importanceofphilosophy.com/Evil_SubjectiveValue.html.
Lewis, C.S. *Mere Christianity*. New York: Macmillan, 1984.
———. *Miracles*. New York: Macmillan, 1978.
Little, William, H.W. Fowler, and J. Coulson. *The Oxford Universal Dictionary on Historical Principles*. Oxford: Clarendon, 1955.
Mackie, J.L. *Ethics: Inventing Right and Wrong*. London: Penguin, 1990.
Markos, Louis A. "Myth Matters." *Christianity Today*, April 23, 2001, https://www.christianitytoday.com/ct/2001/april23/1.32.html.
Martin, Terence. *The Instructed Vision*. Bloomington: Indiana University Press, 1961.
McGinn, Colin. *The Character of Mind: An Introduction to the Philosophy of Mind*. Oxford: Oxford University Press, 1998.
McGrath, Alister. *The Dawkins Delusion*. London: SPCK, 2007.
Meyer, Stephen C. *Signature in the Cell: DNA and the Evidence for Intelligent Design*. New York: HarperCollins, 2009.
Migeod, F.W.H. *Aspects of Evolution*. London: Heath Cranton, 1932.
Miller, Ed L. *Believing in God: Readings on Faith and Reason*. Upper Saddle River, NJ: Prentice-Hall, 1996.
Miller, John E. *Laura Ingalls Wilder's Little Town: Where History and Literature Meet*. Lawrence: University of Kansas Press, 1994.

Bibliography

Milton, Richard. *The Facts of Life: Shattering the Myth of Darwinism*. London: Quality Paperbacks, 1992.
Nagel, Thomas. *What Does It All Mean? A Very Short Introduction to Philosophy*. Oxford: Oxford University Press, 1987.
Norman, Richard. *The Moral Philosophers: An Introduction to Ethics*. Oxford: Oxford University Press, 1998.
Otto, Rudolf. *The Idea of the Holy: An Inquiry into the Non-Rational Factor in the Idea of the Divine and its Relation to the Rational*. Translated by John W. Harvey. London: Oxford University Press, 1970.
Owens, Joseph. *A History of Ancient Western Philosophy*. New York: Appleton, Century, and Crofts, 1959.
Park, Robert. *Voodoo Science*. Oxford: Oxford University Press, 2000.
Paton, H.J. *The Moral Law: Kant's Groundwork of the Metaphysics of Morals*. London: Hutchinson University Library, 1961.
Pearcey, Nancy. "Darwin Meets the Berenstain Bears: Evolution as a Total Worldview." In *Uncommon Dissent*, edited by William A. Dembski, 53–74. Wilmington, DE: ISI, 2004.
Peirce, Charles Sanders. "The Ways of Justifying Belief. In *Readings in Philosophy*, edited by John Herman Randall, Jr., Justus Buchler, and Evelyn Urban Shirk, 30–43. New York: Barnes and Noble, 1967.
Penrose, Roger. *Shadows of the Mind*. London: Vintage Random House, 1994.
Pinker, Steven. "The Brain: The Mystery of Consciousness." *Time,* January 29, 2007, http://content.time.com/time/magazine/article/0,9171,1580394,00.html.
Plato. *The Collected Dialogues of Plato*. Bollingen Series LXXI. Edited by Edith Hamilton and Huntington Cairns. Princeton: Princeton University Press, 1961.
Randall, John Herman, Justus Buchler, and Evelyn Urban Shirk. *Readings in Philosophy*. New York: Barnes and Noble, 1967.
Ridley, Matt. *The Origins of Virtue*. London: Viking, 1996.
Russell, Bertrand. *Religion and Science*. London: Oxford University Press. 1949.
Satris, Stephen. *Taking Sides: Clashing Views on Controversial Moral Issues*. Guilford, CT: Dushkin/McGraw-Hill, 2000.
Schick, Theodore, Jr. "Morality Requires God . . . or Does It?" *Free Inquiry* 17 (Summer1997).https://secularhumanism.org/1997/06/morality-requires-god-or-does-it/.
Schleiermacher, Friedrich. *On Religion: Speeches to its Cultured Despisers*. Translated by John Oman. New York: Harper, 1958.
Schutzenberger, Marcel-Paul. "The Miracles of Darwinism." In *Uncommon Dissent*, edited by William A. Dembski, 41–52. Wilmington, DE: ISI, 2004.
Semogas, Kathryn and Suzanne Dhaliwal. "Topic #A3 – Xenophanes: Poet and Sage." www.chass.utoronto.ca/~dhutchin/s14b.htm
Singh, Jagjit. *Great Ideas of Modern Mathematics*. New York: Dover, 1959.
Sisson, Edward. "Teaching the Flaws in Neo-Darwinism." In *Uncommon Dissent*, edited by William A. Dembski, 75–98. Wilmington, DE: ISI, 2004.

Bibliography

Stapledon, Olaf. *Philosophy and Living*. Harmondsworth, Middlesex: Penguin, 1939.
Stewart, Ian. *Life's Other Secret: The New Mathematics of the Living World*. London: Penguin, 1999.
Strunk, Orlo, ed. *Readings in the Psychology of Religion*. New York: Abingdon, 1959.
Swinburne, Richard. *The Evolution of the Soul*. Oxford: Clarendon, 1997.
Teilhard de Chardin, Pierre. *Science and Christ*. Translated by Rene Hague. London: Collins, 1965.
Thagard, Paul. "Ethical Coherence." *Philosophical Psychology* 11 (1998) 405–22. https://www.tandfonline.com/doi/abs/10.1080/09515089808573270.
Tipler, Frank J. "Refereed Journals: Do They Insure Quality or Enforce Orthodoxy?" In *Uncommon Dissent*, edited by William A. Dembski, 115–30. Wilmington, DE: ISI, 2004.
Tolkien, J.R.R. "Beowulf: The Monsters and the Critics." In *Beowulf: A Verse Translation*, edited by Daniel Donoghue, 103–30. Translated by Seamus Heaney. New York; London: Norton, 2002.
Toulmin, Stephen. *The Philosophy of Science*. London: Arrow, 1962.
Trefil, James and Robert M. Hazen. *The Sciences: An Integrated Approach*. New York: John Wiley, 2000.
Trueblood, D. Elton. *Philosophy of Religion*. New York: Harper, 1957.
Walsh, John E. *Unravelling Piltdown: The Science Fraud of the Century and Its Solution*. London: The Softback Preview, 1997.
Westaway, F. W. *Science in the Dock: Guilty or Not Guilty?* London: Blackie, 1942.
White, A. J. Monty. *Wonderfully Made*. Durham, England: Evangelical, 1989.
Whittaker, John H. *Matters of Faith and Matters of Principle: Religious Truth Claims and Their Logic*. San Antonio: Trinity University Press, 1981.
Winston, Robert. *What Makes Me Me?* London: Dorling Kindersley, 2004.
Wolfe, Susan. *Freedom Within Reason*. Oxford: Oxford University Press, 1990.
Wright, Robert. "Essay: The Brain: How We Make Life and Death Decisions." *Time*, January 29, 2007, http://content.time.com/time/magazine/article/0,9171,1580372,00.html.

www.ingramcontent.com/pod-product-compliance
Lightning Source LLC
Chambersburg PA
CBHW070931160426
43193CB00011B/1647